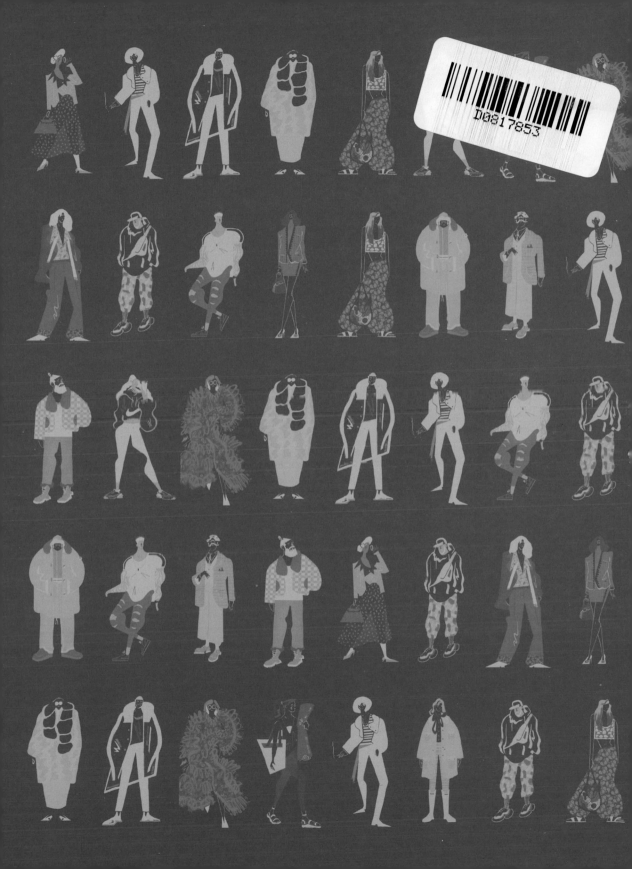

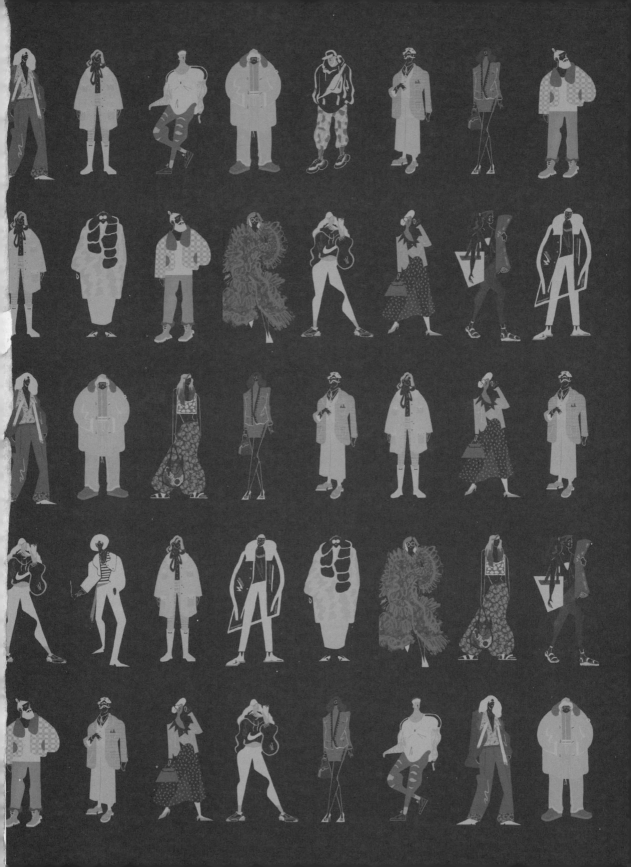

F*SHION WANKERS

IT TAKES ONE TO KNOW ONE

F*SHION WANKERS

IT TAKES ONE TO KNOW ONE

MARCUS JAYE

AMMONITE
PRESS

CONTENTS

GET A GRIP ON FASHION

EMBRACING YOUR INNER FASHION WANKER

FASHION WANKER BINGO

SPOT THE FASHION WANKER

FASHION WANKERS

IT TAKES ONE TO KNOW ONE...

The Chic Geek

Fashion Wanker (n.):
A confident fashion
obsessive.

Fashion Wankers was
written in recognition of,
and in response to, the
contemporary fashion
characters I continually see around me. It is a celebration
of the types of fashionistas – and fashionistos – who
populate and illuminate our real and digital worlds. Being
called a Fashion Wanker is not a criticism, it's a badge of
honour. It's about celebrating your love of fashion and all
its ridiculousness. Fashion thrives on these special
Wankers and needs all their energy and passion to
continue on its journey.

We're currently living in the Age of Bonkers (see page 34),
Tom Ford's 'Fucking Fabulous' and dick pics, so we sure as
hell can call ourselves Fashion Wankers. Seriously, being a
Fashion Wanker is a good thing. Whether you are already
one, know one, love one, are related to one or aspire to be
one, then this book is for you.

In the first half, you'll be shown how to maximize your Fashion Wanker status by learning the lingo, know-how and all the insider info to hold your own at the fashion party you've just crashed. Oops!

In the second half, you'll identify differing facets of your personality (and many others), by learning to recognize the tribal traits and accessories of contemporary Fashion Wanker characters – and the ones that go into making the original that is YOU.

Along the way, you'll discover the do's and don'ts of navigating the confusing world of style and fashion, led by the indomitable Chic Geek. (Don't worry, he'll help you see the wood for the Dries… Soz.)

You'll learn to take the piss out of yourself as well as others, to ignore the resting bitch faces of those who envy your swagger and to push yourself out of your stylistic comfort zone. All Fashion Wankers deserve their place in the fashion ecosystem regardless of their position in the fabulous fashion food chain.

So, if you think Blockchain is jewellery, Mugatu's piano key necktie was one of the defining moments in fashion design and PrettyLittleThing would be better being named UglyBigThing, then you're welcome here with open arms. When somebody says you look like a right Fashion Wanker, take it as the ultimate compliment! Own it. Werk it.

Never be BORING. Promise me.

Kisses,
Marcus Jaye

THE CHIC GEEK

AN INTRODUCTION TO...

When I started my blog, The Chic Geek, in 2009, little did I know where my love of fashion and its crazy unpredictability would take me. The Chic Geek has since grown to become one of the UK's most recognizable and respected online men's media brands. The Chic Geek character was born out of my shyness in front of a camera and by donning an oversized papier-mâché head he became bigger than me. While we both share red hair and geek glasses, he is far more knowledgable, entertaining and handsome than I could ever be…

From the early years of blogging through to the rise of social media, the fashion world has grown exponentially and has resonated far beyond its traditional boundaries. I'm just bobbing along for the ride.

What all this experience has given me is the confidence to trust my intuition. If you are to be a style leader, then you do not have the time to wait for the facts. Fashion is, after all, subjective and you have to learn to trust your gut instinct on what is good and when to run with it, and not be afraid of sticking your neck out.

What is fashion?

Fashion is part of everything we do. It goes far beyond the clothes we wear. It's the words we use, the places we go and even what we eat. Today, fashion designers are some of the world's biggest celebrities where even their cats and dogs can become mega stars – I'm looking at you Choupette & Neville – and fashion brands are now some of the world's biggest companies.

Fashion is a serious business, employing many millions of people globally. But, it's also important to accept and recognize the ludicrous and ephemeral nature of it all. Style, on the other hand, is something else entirely. Think of it like a muscle, it needs to be constantly exercised. Let me help. You're going to have to do some heavy lifting to define your own personal style. It takes work, but it's well worth it.

The insatiable beast of fashion is everywhere and, regardless of price point and location, we can all have a go at taming it.

This is your journey, your fashion Tough Mudder.

#FashionWankers of the world unite!

GET A GRIP ON FASHION

WHY FASHION
MATTERS

What exactly is 'fashion', anyway? It's the prevailing style at any given time and it doesn't stay still: it's about constant change. In the past it was about people wanting to show off their bling, class and status; it was the means by which they stayed one step ahead of the great unwashed. Today, though, it's more about showing off your personality and creativity, while simultaneously referencing that you know what's 'in fashion'. Simply by buying new clothes you're taking part in fashion, whether you like it or not.

Some people see fashion as being silly and frivolous, and it makes them a more serious person if they dismiss it or play it down. Big mistake! All that says is that they don't fully understand or feel confident about fashion, so they distance themselves from taking risks to avoid feeling like they're going to fall flat on their faces in some way. Instead they find comfort in proclaiming their ignorance, belittling fashion and opting out.

We all wear clothes and we all make choices when we go shopping or put something on. Even if someone thinks that they always wear the same black t-shirt and jeans, over time, as those basics are replaced with new, the cut will change – even if only in tiny ways – and you'll see subtle differences. These small changes are part of the obsessive march of fashion; they enable us to date old photos, even if the people in them might have said they weren't particularly fashion conscious.

Fashion doesn't happen on its own: the industry is a huge global business with a self-interest in continual change. It's ultimately about getting us to buy more stuff. Fashion looks to tastemakers to show the way. These people, whether designers or people working at a brand, make decisions which ripple out to the wider audience and to other brands. Remember that 'cerulean blue' moment in *The Devil Wears Prada*? Fashion used to filter top down, but, now, it's more unpredictable, coming from the street or social media.

Designers face incredible pressure to match up creativity with commercial success. If your main business is making and selling suits, for example, you'll always want tailoring to come back into fashion. But, at the same time, you'll need to offer the suit shape and style that's fashionable at that moment in time. Respect to those who can manage both to make great clothes and to generate money.

Humans are naturally inquisitive, we get bored and desire change. Fashion is about novelty. We're basically buying ideas. What you feel today, could or will be very different to how you feel in a year's time. Fashion Wankers follow their instincts, but also keep their ears and eyes open. Listen and watch other wankers but, ultimately, make your own decisions.

Remember, fashion should be fun. If it's not, you're doing it wrong.

HOW TO SHOP

People often ask me for help with their style, or to tell them what's 'in'. It's as if they expect me to sum it up in one easy sentence. It just doesn't work like that. I mean, how long have you got?!!

NEVER BE SEDUCED BY A LABEL

Being snobby about labels is very old-fashioned and, most of the time, buying expensive brands means you've probably spent a lot of money to not look that good, which is kinda dumb...okay!

The best way to help somebody shop is to edit their choices. Just like releasing an animal back into the wild, let them roam and run free. If it's in a shop or online, get them to decide what they think works and come back with their selections. (This is also much less work, easier and quicker).

There is no point putting somebody in something they feel uncomfortable in, even if you think they look good: they won't wear it, so it will be a waste of time and money. Much better to edit the stuff they've chosen that fits in with their natural self-image; all you have to do is say 'yes' or 'no' to their selection.

THE CHIC GEEK SAYS...

"If you don't love it, don't buy it. I bet there are plenty of items in your wardrobe with the labels still on."

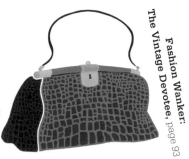

Handbags are just for girls? What a croc of shit!

Fashion Wanker: The Vintage Devotee, page 93

IF YOU'RE NOT LUCKY ENOUGH TO HAVE YOUR OWN CHIC
GEEK TO TAKE YOU SHOPPING, YOU CAN OPERATE
AS YOUR OWN STYLIST-COME-EDITOR. JUST FOLLOW
THESE POINTERS:

- **Don't rush. But if you spot something you really like, move quickly before it sells out.**

- Take risks. New styles often call for a period of adjustment. If you only wore clothes that felt immediately comfortable, you'd never move forward. Stay true to yourself, but give new styles a chance.

- **Trust the mirror. Learn to look at yourself objectively and be realistic about who you are, not who you'd like to be.**

- Look ahead. Think about where and when you'd wear something now. If you can't visualize a scenario, put it back on the rack.

- **Take care. Look at the label and see what it's made from, where it was made and how to care for it. This will also help you to assess how much you'd be willing to pay for it and if you're prepared to put the effort in to care for it.**

- Don't get suckered into 'bargains'. It's not a saving if it stays in the closet. Conversely, you can afford to be more experimental if something doesn't cost a lot.

- **Do your homework. Check out the designers behind the brands so you know whose taste you're buying into. If there's a designer you really love keep track of their movements (don't wait outside their home!), so you know when they jump ship to another design house.**

- Start at home. It's not always about buying new. True Fashion Wankers start with an inventory of what they have, edit it down and recycle or give away what they no longer need before hitting the shops.

AIN'T WHAT YOU SAY, IT'S THE WAY THAT YOU SAY IT

Don't let yourself look like an amateur. *Eyeroll*.
Knowing how to pronounce specific labels, designers
and brands will allow you to seamlessly segue yourself
into any Fashion Wankers company. Read, repeat and
don't f*ck it up!

Ann Demeulemeester – *ann de-mule-eh-meester*
One of the famous Antwerp Six designers.
Serious fashion in dark colours for the fashion goth.

Audemars Piguet – *oh-duh-mahr pea-gay*
Swiss manufacturer of expensive wristwear,
founded in 1875.

Azzedine Alaïa – *azz-eh-deen a-liar*
Tunisian-born couturier, known particularly
for his much-imitated body-con designs of
the 1980s. Since his death, Maison Alaïa
continues production.

Balenciaga – *bah-len-see-ah-gah*
Fashion house, feted during the heyday of its
Spanish founder, Cristobal Balenciaga, now headed
up by Fashion Wankers favourite Demna Gvasalia
(that's *deem-na vas-ah-liya*).

Balmain – *bahl-mahhhhn*
Old-school French fashion house showcasing classic
Parisian style with look-at-me embellishment.

Bottega Veneta – *bow-tay-guh vah-netta*
Italian luxury goods brand, famous for its
'Intrecciato' (woven) leather bags.

Breguet – *breh-gay*
Luxury Swiss watches from 1775.

Cartier – *kar-t-ey*
Diamonds, daaaarling!!! Jewellery for the seriously minted, founded in Paris in 1847.

Cerruti – *ch-ru-ti*
Italian menswear brand known for its tailoring.

Chanel – *shu-nel*
The ultimate French womenswear label, founded by Coco Chanel in 1910 and going strong (almost) ever since, most recently under Karl Lagerfeld. RIP.

Chopard – *show-par*
Glitzy Swiss watches and jewellery.

Christian Louboutin – *christian loo-boo-tan*
Shoe designer, known for his high-glamour heels with their signature red soles.

Dolce & Gabbana – *dol-chey and gab-ana*
Italian design duo known for their sexy Sicilian looks.

Dries Van Noten – *drees van know-ten*
Celebrated Belgian designer known for his avant-garde use of colour and prints.

Ermenegildo Zegna *er-me-ne-geel-do zen-ya*
Italian fabric producer and luxury menswear brand.

Façonnable – *fa-so-nah-bluh*
Clothing brand founded in a tailor's shop in Nice, France, in 1950. They have been exporting the French Riviera ever since.

Givenchy – *jzhiv-von-shee*
French house, founded by Hubert de Givenchy; much loved by Audrey Hepburn.

Goyard – *go-yah*
The thinking person's Louis Vuitton – luxury luggage and leather goods.

Hermès – *er-mez*
Seriously expensive French leather goods company, famous for its orange packaging.

Hublot – *ooh-blow*
Another Swiss luxury watch brand but of a more recent vintage, founded in 1980.

Jaeger-LeCoultre – *zhay-zhay le coolt ruh*
More watches – but these ones are designed to flip to face the wrist to protect them when you play polo.

Lanvin – *lahn-vahn*
Founded by Jeanne Lanvin in 1889, it is the oldest French fashion house still in operation.

Loewe – *loh-wev-eh*
Spanish luxury goods house, not to be confused with the German electronics company.

Moncler – *mon-kler*
Originally a French sportswear company, it is known for its luxe ski-inspired down jackets and coats.

Moschino – *moss-ski-no*
Playful Italian designer brand – look for handbags or perfume shaped like everyday household objects.

Miu Miu – *mew-mew*
Prada's younger and more decorative sister.

Nike – *ni-key*
Giant American sportswear company.

Paul Smith
Fooled you! As he sounds, and one of the nicest men in fashion.

Ralph Lauren – *Lauren, like the girl's name, NOT Lo-REN like the actress.*
The king of American preppy style.

Rochas – *row-shahs*
A fashion and perfume house, founded in 1925 by French designer Marcel Rochas.

Schiaparelli *skap-a-rel-ee*
Italian couturier known for her surrealist designs; her influence still lingers. Lobster, anybody?!

Versace – *vur-sah-chee*
Italian brand known for its rich, baroque designs, managed by the indomitable Donatella Versace.

Vilebrequin – *vil-bra-ken*
French fashion brand, founded in St Tropez in the 1970s, and still known for its colourful swim shorts.

Yves Saint Laurent – *eve san lau-ron*
The golden boy of French fashion whose house remains highly popular despite losing the 'Yves'.

FASHION HISTORY FOR (SHOP)
DUMMIES

When Adam confidently picked a large fig leaf to cover his modesty (oo-er!), fashion's ever-spinning wheels were set in motion. Whether or not you believe in the Old Testament, fashion and clothing are as old as us losing our hair suits and standing up straight. Clothing and, later, fashion was once a signifier of status, giving a visual message to others with regards to the wearer's wealth and social standing. In the twentieth century this began to change and fashion has since become a reflection of the times and source of an individual's expression. So here's a brief history of the last century to help you bullshit your way through:

THE 1900s

For women, the Victorian hourglass of the previous century was replaced by a romantic S-shaped female silhouette. A high-waisted bodiced blouse and long, full skirt gave a striking pigeon-like shape to the women of the day. The look was often accessorized with a wide-brimmed hat and parasol. Very *My Fair Lady*!

For men, the new Edwardian age was led by King Edward VII who was quite the dresser, so much so that he is the reason why the famous Glenurquhart black-and-white check was renamed the Prince of Wales check. His famous style choices included wearing tweed, Homburg hats and Norfolk jackets. Unheard of at the time, he also opted to leave the bottom button of his coat undone, though his 48-inch waist may have also had a say in the matter.

THE 1910s

The time of women's suffrage and the Great War was a moment when the constriction of previous decades was loosened and dressing became more relaxed. The gilded age and opulence of Edwardian style was replaced by a more practical and freeing approach to fashion. Waists started to drop and it was a transition period for the subsequent Jazz Age of the 1920s.

Women's empowerment was reflected in their dress, giving them the physical freedom that their clothing had previously lacked. The Great War had an impact on fashion, with timeless items like the trench coat resonating out into wider society.

Women's fashion, 1910s

Louise Brooks, 1920s

THE 1920s

Arguably the most glamorous decade of the 20th century, this was the time when fashion modernized. Women's clothing continued to react to the cultural and social changes of the era, and gave us many of the items we still wear today. Black lost the shackles of mourning and became a simple and elegant way to dress. Coco Chanel's 'Little Black Dress' was part of this movement. Revolutionary at the time, it was described by *Vogue* as 'Chanel's Ford' and was easily replicated at every price point.

Men's fashion looked to the Duke of Windsor, the future King, for his use of pattern and colour and his playful approach to tailoring.

THE 1930s

The elegance of the 1930s was summed up with the invention of the bias-cut dress. By cutting the fabric at a 45-degree angle across the warp and weft – the vertical and horizontal threads in a fabric – the resulting greater stretch gives the fabric more movement and the ability to hug the body and curves. It helped to invent the silver screen image of shimmering, long satin dresses and elegant, wavy hair for women. The addition of a zipper became widely used for the first time and was a precursor to the forthcoming practical fashions, as the dark clouds of war started to form.

Miriam Battista, 1932

Christian Dior Dress, 1947

THE 1940s

The austerity of the 1940s created an atmosphere of make do and mend. Fashion became a reflection of the time, with women's fashion being heavily influenced by menswear and the new roles they were fulfilling during the war effort.

Post-war Paris became the epicentre of fashion and what Paris said, went. Christian Dior's revolutionary 'New Look' in 1947 set the world alight. The calf-length full skirt and cinched-in waist created a boom in Parisian couture, which continued well into the following decade.

THE 1950s

The 1950s was a feminine confection of florals and polka dots in full-skirted and tea-length shapes, all accessorized with pill-box hats and box bags. This was very 'together' dressing.

Coco Chanel invented her famous bouclé tweed two-piece suit with boxy jacket and fitted skirt. A look which still resonates today.

For men, young, youth tribes emerged. In Britain, Teddy Boys dressed in their Edwardian velvet-collared coats and crepe-soled shoes emulating their heroes of the day. In the US, Elvis, James Dean and Marlon Brando went for the bad-boy look, with their quiffs and leather jackets.

James Dean, 1955

Mary Quant Minidress, 1969

THE 1960s

The 'Swinging Sixties' saw the post-war baby-boomer generation become teenagers and their desire to be different from their parents meant that fashion got creative. Designers and brands saw the future of fashion in 'ready-to-wear'. Women's sexual liberation, the space race and hippie culture was represented in Mary Quant's revealing mini-skirt, Paco Rabanne's metallic shift dresses and Yves Saint Laurent's Mondrian dress.

Menswear became Modish. A movement dictated by the clean lines and slim-fit of Italian style and tailoring, café culture and jazz.

THE 1970s

A decade of extremes, the 1970s took us from the tail end of hippie into glam rock, on to disco and finally ending with punk. The flared trousers and wide lapels of its menswear are all thanks to London tailor to the stars, Tommy Nutter. Dressing three of the four Beatles on the famous *Abbey Road* cover, not to mention Elton John, Nutter pioneered a strongly-shouldered suit in bold patterns and colours which resonated from the late 1960s and throughout the subsequent decade.

The anti-establishment and anarchic punk movement bookended the decade with threatening looks of safety pins, bondage trousers and metal studs.

Sex Pistols, 1979

Kate O'Mara and Joan Collins, 1981

THE 1980s

The 1980s saw the explosion in designer brands, and fashion was denoted by large shoulder pads and even bigger hair. This was the beginning of fashion's huge growth, from a closed and exclusive industry out into wider popular culture, making some designers as famous as the celebrities they dressed. This was the start of the fashion mega brand. Power dressing reflected a decade obsessed with money. Television shows like *Dallas* and *Dynasty* gave the 'greed is good' idea extra credibility thanks to expensive and decadent clothes worn by the 'supermodels' of the day.

THE 1990s

The 1990s were a time of minimalism. For women, 'heroin chic' became the look, thanks to model Kate Moss. Designers promoted underwear as outerwear with simple lace-trimmed slip dresses. Music had a big impact on fashion during this decade, with menswear going 'grunge' in the footsteps of Kurt Cobain, and house music and rave culture producing relaxed and casual clothing for long nights and weekends in Ibiza.

Alexander McQueen emerged as one of the greatest designers of the century, illustrating through his immersive shows and designs how fashion can become art.

Kate Moss, 1993

Alexander McQueen A/W, Paris Fashion Week, 2011

THE 2000s

At the turn of the millennium, fashion was as big as it has ever been and designer fashion became increasingly more accessible thanks to collaborations between the designers and affordable retailers.

Reality television stars and the internet were having a huge influence on people's fashion decisions, as well as how they were consuming and buying clothes. In menswear, fashion became super skinny and shrunken thanks to designers such as Thom Browne and Hedi Slimane, and musicians such as Pete Doherty.

WHAT IS STYLE?

It's subjective, of course: 'style' is one of those big/little words which means different things to different people. When people talk of somebody having style, they are often referring to an image they've seen, usually a celebrity, which captures the subject in that moment and resonates into fashion history. But it's more than that.

For you, it's the choices you make when you put something on. Those choices are an expression of your taste and a barometer of your level of sophistication and creativity. The long game in style and fashion is to show that you're sophisticated while still being yourself, yet looking contemporary and fashionable at the same time. It may take some juggling!

Dress in the now. How you feel today. This minute. Not looking ahead or trying to overthink it. Be yourself, everybody else is taken (One of history's greatest Fashion Wankers once said that).

THE CHIC GEEK SAYS...

"Take the piss out of yourself! A truly stylish person will be the first person to poke fun at themselves. This is a knowing confidence and the acknowledgment that it should be fun and the opposite of serious."

STYLE ISN'T FASHION

Fashion is the range of contemporary choices available to you; style is the choices you make to reflect your personality or how you feel that day. These two are bedfellows, and while you can ignore fashion, you must never ignore style!

STYLE IS:

- Getting the best thing from even the worst shop or website.

- **Taking risks and playing with how you look.**

- Sometimes thinking you look stupid, while in fact you look cool.

- **Not about looking different for the sake of it.**

- Acknowledging fashion trends, making them your own and taking them up a notch. Tiptoeing along that uber stylish tightrope!

- **Only trying to impress yourself.**

- Staying flexible. Style is an attitude and it can change.

- **Having confidence. This may take some longer than others. You don't have to rush it.**

- Not projecting your style insecurities onto others. You can have an opinion, but don't be a bitch. PLEASE!

- **Taking feedback only from those whose style you respect – ignore all the others.**

- Being elastic. Style is constantly changing, so learn how to adapt.

- **Making Quality Street look like Dover Street. You don't need to spend big to be stylish.**

A GUIDE TO
MATERIALS & PRINTS

When it comes to materials, fabrics and patterns, a Fashion Wanker's choices are limitless and never-ending. By picking the interesting, the colourful and the creative, in the right combination, you'll soon shoot up the chart of best-dressed and most interesting individuals.

Materials are the raw goods from which fabrics are made. Fabrics are the way in which those materials are woven or printed, and patterns are the decoration. Here are some of the major options:

RAW MATERIALS

Cotton is the thirstiest of natural fibres – it takes a lot of water to produce. Cotton's popularity is thanks to its versatility and soft handle. It sprouts soft cotton balls from the *Gossypium* plant and is used in everything from T-shirts to denim jeans. **Wool** is the umbrella term for hair fibres obtained from animals, but we traditionally think of sheep. Wool is a great fibre for outerwear when woven into winter coats or knitted into cardigans and jumpers. When blowing the budget, we dream of cashmere, which is the hair from under the neck of goats. Cashmere is good at holding coloured dyes and is best bought in striking tones.
Silk is the smoothest of fibres, spun from the cocoons of silkworms. The fashion world is always hungry for it and it's mass-produced in India, China and the Far East – as well as, perhaps more surprisingly, Brazil and Iran. The beautiful sheen and lightness lends itself to evening- and occasion-wear seen under candlelight.
Linen is a fibre taken from the flax plant which is grown in temperate climates to keep you cool and

Fashion Wanker: The Know-It-All, page 87

DOES IT COME IN PLAID?

fresh in warmer ones. Linen is often seen in menswear in shirts and suiting for summertime. Just try and keep those creases out. **Man-made materials** such as Lycra, nylon, polyester, acetate and acrylic are produced from chemicals. The benefit of these materials is that they reach the parts that natural ones can't reach, so they're ideal for stretching and anything to do with athleisure or sports.

FABRICS

Jacquard is a fabric with the design woven into the fabric rather than printed on it. The design is within the fabric which increases its durability and makes it read like a braille of fabric designs. Often used in suiting and more tailored garments. **Satin** is a weave that typically has a glossy surface and a dull back. Silk satin is the more expensive option and is perfect for bias-cut eveningwear or the lapels on a tuxedo. **Jersey** is a fabric that is knitted rather than woven, which gives the end result a degree of give or stretch. Although it's usually cotton, it's also sometimes made from man-made, silk or wool. This is the heart of your slobbing-out-watching-box-sets wardrobe. **Velvet** is a type of woven tufted fabric with a short, dense pile. It can be made from cotton, silk or synthetic. It holds colours very deeply so works well in black or navy in eveningwear or ribbon-like accessories. **Corduroy** is a soft textile with a distinct 'cord' or wale running through it. This is the fabric of kings and geography teachers… **Tweed** is a woollen fabric with a plain weave, twill or herringbone design and stems from the British countryside. This robust and hard-working fabric was made for the hunting, shooting and fishing crowd to keep them warm and protected outdoors. Tally-ho! **Denim** is made from cotton twill, and is mostly used for jeans. The warp thread is dyed, while the weft thread is left white and

is why you get those annoying, dangly white bits when you slash your jeans or make a hole. **Tulle** is a very fine, stiff netting and it can be made of silk, nylon, polyester and rayon. It has recently become a designer favourite for garments with volume. It's perfect for princess dressing.

PATTERNS

Paisley was originally from Persia, but this teardrop design was renamed after a town in Scotland which became renowned for its Paisley shawls. It later became a design associated with psychedelia and the Free-Love movement of the late 1960s. **Intarsia** sounds like a queen from *Rupaul's Drag Race*. It is a knitting technique where the design is pieced together like a jigsaw using multiple colours. Think of your mum's furry cat jumper from the 1980s. **Polka dot** is a pattern consisting of an array of circular dots and is named after the popular 'polka' dance. **Geometric** is abstract designs such as diagonals, grids, stripes or any shapes in rigid and structured patterns. The Italian house of Missoni is famous for its colourful geometric patterns. **Animal** Teach me tiger, or cheetah, or zebra. Stunning, stylish animal prints will see you join the archive at Serengeti-images. Grrrr… **Camouflage** is the art of concealment and usually means the army type of greens, greys and blacks. Many brands have co-opted camouflage with far from subtle colours and patterns to do the reverse and get you noticed. **Florals** Hawaiian to chintz, florals are for all year round, not just spring. Groundbreaking. From tiny Liberty Tana Lawn designs to bold tropical hibiscus, there are as many floral designs as flowers. **Checks** Can I get the check?! Plaids, tartans, ginghams, tattersalls, who doesn't love checks, mate? **Tartan** is associated with Scotland and was made fashionable by the Victorians with every clan having their own distinct pattern.

"Before you leave the house, look in the mirror and take one thing off."

Coco Chanel
(Note, this doesn't apply to swimwear!)

SLIDING INTO YOUR DMS & OTHER FOOTWEAR

Shoes, glorious shoes. It's no wonder that self-acknowledged Fashion Wankers have become addicted to footwear. Shoes are some of the most democratic items in fashion, with body shape and gender rarely holding back your options. From the mink-lined slide to the winklepicker, and the Chelsea boot to Alexander McQueen's iconic Armadillo, there are as many styles as blisters... Ouch!

THE CHIC GEEK SAYS...

"Put the YOU into shoe, you've got sole!"

Fashion Wanker: The Basic, page 95

The Ugg was going to be called the Beaut, but then somebody looked at it...

#FashionWankers are always well shod. From Sneakerheads to Shoeaholics, whatever the style or the material, from crocodile to vegan, choose well and make sure your feet talk the walk. Here's a speedy rundown of the main footwear styles:

Flats (as a pancake) They range from 'ballet flats' (round toe and thin sole) to (slightly) more daring pointy-toed versions. **Heels** Love 'em or hate them, they're the ones you need to feel elevated. They'll give you a lift, whether you want an extra inch or eight From skyscraper stilettos to more manageable kitten heels to solid Cuban heels, we can all do with feeling that little bit taller sometimes. **Wedges/Platforms** Shoes in which one piece of material serves as both the sole and the heel. 'Flatforms' leave your feet relatively flat on a platform, other styles are essentially heels with the sole gap between the heel and toe filled in. **Sandals** It's one of the oldest footwear styles: a simple

construction of sole and straps. From gladiator to thong to sturdy Birkenstocks, they ensure that your feet get to see the sun, so make sure they're prepared. Hello! **Boots** Covering not only the feet but also the ankles up to the knee or even higher. Available in any and every style, from delicate stilettos to chunky Dr. Martens. 'Fuck Me Boots' will even go up to the thigh, but it's more of an attitude than a style. **Lace-ups** As described; shoes with laces. They're often relatively sober 'smart' shoes, made from leather and flat-soled with a small heel. Think Oxfords, Derbies and classic brogues. (If you want the sobriety but not the laces, monkstraps have a buckled strap over the top of the foot). **Sneakers** No definition needed: the contemporary comfort shoe of choice and a massive style indicator with millions of options, whether you're actually headed for the gym or just pretending. **Loafers** Slip-on shoes, including moccasins and boat shoes. The most famous – not least for its longevity – is probably Gucci's snaffle loafer inspired by a horse bit.

31

EMBRACING YOUR INNER FASHION WANKER

THE AGE OF
BONKERS

We're living in a very exciting time: a time when, fashion-wise, anything goes. It's the Age of Bonkers. The maximalist Guccification of the fashion world has stretched its boundaries and made it possible for each and every gender to step up their style and embrace the more-is-more look.

Über stylish or Uber driver?

These street style Fashion Wankers were papped during fashion week. The best catwalk can often be found outside the main shows.

Fashion Wanker:
The Sneaker Geek, page 109

FANNY PACK... *if you live stateside*

You don't need anyone's permission to wear any look you choose, but seeing other people push the fashion envelope – and appreciating how good they can look – has a knock-on effect. If all the world really is a stage, then make sure that you're a player – life's the drama and you're the star. The fashion spectrum is the widest it has ever been, so if you opt to flake out in a tracksuit, at least make sure it's a lurex one.

Accessories are one outlet for our desire to leave a distinctive impression, in both our real and our virtual lives. Look to eyewear, hats, jewellery and shoes to help you look like you've just stepped out of a Wes Anderson movie or a Frida Kahlo painting, even if you're just popped out for a pint of milk.

Bonkers is a good thing, so liberate yourself. Accessories are your props and your attitude of confidence will be magnetic to others. Even if you don't always quite hit the spot, who cares? The ones who matter will be impressed.

Fashion Wankers know their own. They're the opposite of boring.

FASHION WANKER
LINGO

The gift of the gab will take you from basic bitch to chic geek. Real Fashion Wankers are making this shit up all the time. Here's a starter set of well-established sayings to get you up to speed and, soon, you'll be fluent in fashion B.S. like the best of us.

AOP All-over print. **Athleisure** Casual clothes which take their inspiration from gym wear. **Basic** Double meaning to this one – first, a description of those simple items in your closet, like tees, plain shirts and trousers, or second, a description of you, if you're not on top of the latest language and trends. **BNWT** Brand new with tags. Often used to describe second-hand and unworn stuff on eBay. **Bumster** Low-rise hipster trousers which show your bum crack. Originally one of Alexander McQueen's inspired creations. **Caping** Wearing your jacket or coat over your shoulders like a cape. Some people think it makes them more 'fashion'. They're often wrong. **Capsule collection** An edited group of clothes to offer a full wardrobe in the smallest number of pieces. **Creator** AKA an influencer. They create 'content'. **Die** A reaction to something really, really good. As in, 'I die for that' or 'To die for'. Also used for the same effect: 'Dead'. **Drops** When fashion brands and designers 'drop' limited-edition product at regular intervals to create hype and demand. Drops can be flipped (see **flipping**). **Everything** Melodramatic way of saying that you like something. **#FashionWankers** People who celebrate and own their love of fashion. **Fashionista** A female follower of fashion. (The male is **Fashionisto**). **Fierce** A way of describing something that is really good. **Flipping** When you buy something that has been produced in limited numbers and sell it on at a profit. **Frow** The front row at a fashion show. **Giving you life** Something that gets you overexcited. **Groundbreaking** You say this when somebody says or does something really obvious or common, but they think it's really new or different. **Haute Couture** Mega-expensive personally crafted fashion from the couture houses, often in Paris. **Hipster** A person who follows the latest trends and fashions and is under the age of 35. Millennials while they're young. **Hunty** A combination of 'honey' and 'c*nt'. Often shortened to 'hun'. It originated in the drag world as a term of endearment for your friends. **Hypebeast** Somebody who wants the latest clothing, shoes and accessories for the sole purpose of impressing others. **Influencer** Somebody who thinks their opinions or lifestyle is influential on others. **It** Long-established suffix for anything that is widely acknowledged to be enjoying a moment of popularity – for example, an 'It girl', or an 'It bag'. **LBD** Little black dress. **NFI** Not fucking invited. **Ombré** When a colour gradually fades or gets darker over an area of fabric or hair. **On fleek** A combination of sleek and fly: something that is flawless or perfect. **On point** Something that is perfect and exacting. **OOTD** Outfit of the day. Used to tag outfits on Instagram. **OTT** Over the top. **Passè** Fancy way of saying something has gone or is over. **Peng** Fit, hot and/or good-looking. **Pop-up** Usually a shop that's open for a short time on a temporary site. **PPW** Price per wear. Also known as cost per wear. Often used to justify an expensive purchase. **Pre-fall** Designers and brands usually produce two main collections a year. Pre-fall is released before the second main collection and focuses more on wardrobe staples and less on strictly seasonal pieces. **Ready-to-wear** Basically, everyday clothes. People used to have to be patient and wait if they wanted clothes made especially for them. The ready-to-wear

clothes – prêt-à-porter in French – were less exclusive. Haute couture is made to order. Variations include MTM – made to measure – and bespoke. The first is measured to fit, the second offers more scope for choosing the fabric and style. **Realness** The genuine product, the real deal, and so on. A jokey way of being able to pass for something. For example, when making a coffee with your Nespresso machine you might say 'serving some Starbucks barista realness'. **RFID** A clothing label or tag that says when and where the piece was made, and by whom. **Shacket** If a jacket and a shirt had a baby. **Shoefie** A selfie of your shoes. **Slay** To kill, in a style way. Blame RuPaul. **Squad goals** When you have only hot friends and want to show them off. *Eyeroll*. **Sneakerhead** Somebody obsessed with trainers or sneakers. **Unisex** Clothes that don't have a gender. **Zaddy** A man 'with swag' who is attractive and also fashionable.

Those shoes SLAY me

Gucci sneakers, 2018

37

THE ART OF
FASHION ZEN

Fashion is constantly looking to the future, which makes it a truly optimistic industry. Working at least six months ahead, fashion has a glass-half-full attitude, with the premise that the best is yet to come (fingers crossed). It can also be stressful and in our age of over-indulgence, when it comes to our wardrobes, we're at risk of drowning in our own good taste…

THE CHIC GEEK SAYS…

"When the world gives you Lululemon, make lulu-lemonade!"

HERE ARE SOME TIPS TO ACHIEVING FASHION WANKER WARDROBE ZEN:

- Start sorting in the right frame of mind. Do it when you want to, not when you have to.

- **Put some music on. Make it fun. You'll probably discover things you don't remember you owned. This is going to save you a fortune!**

- Take everything out. Don't put anything back until you're sure you'll be keeping it. When you put it back, keep to some kind of order, even if you just divide the space between casual and more formal clothes.

- **Give your wardrobe a good freshen up; dust and vacuum while it's empty.**

- Sort the things you're getting rid of into three categories: toss, sell or donate. It's important we do as much as we can to limit the impact of our waste. Dispose of responsibly.

- **Be as ruthless as you can bear to be. There'll be a few items you'll never want to get rid of, your long-term favourites. But leave some space for those new favourites you haven't met yet.**

- If it doesn't fit, and it's never likely to, it's time to say goodbye. If it is something that somebody else will love, try eBay or a resale site. (More doo-llars for future shopping!

- **If you're not sure, try it on. How does it make you feel? Does it bring you joy? If it still gives you that retail buzz, keep it.**

- Are there any gaps? This is your chance to see if there's anything you actually need, or anything you particularly like and want more of.

- **Think about clearing out your wardrobe in the same way as cleaning up your desktop. You'll feel so much better afterwards.**

- Make 'Meet, Pay, Love' your new shopping mantra.

COMBINING COLOUR

I could spout off some bollocks about colour wheels and complementary colours, but I'm sure you already know that stuff. Colour is not something to be afraid of. Although nobody wants to look like a set from a children's television show, that doesn't mean you shouldn't experiment either.

ANY COLOUR AS LONG AS IT'S NOT BLACK

Colour is not something to be afraid of. It doesn't make you cooler to wear black all of the time. In fact, you probably look like a sales assistant, waiter or security guard. Take your pick. Team colour with colour. If you're wearing strong primaries then add more of the same. It's all about balancing. Trust me, it works.

LATITUDE LIGHTING

Colour works differently in different climates and lights. In northerly countries like the UK, strong, bold colours can look dirty – I'm talking about you, yellow! – while in the south – Spain, Italy, Mexico – they appear clearer and more vibrant. If you want to try a bold colour in a greyer climate it works best to team it with a strong, darker shade – for example, Easyjet orange goes well with dusky grape.

SATURATION POINT

Colour looks different depending on your fabric choice, too. It appears more saturated and stronger in silk and cashmere, while cotton doesn't hold colour so well and quickly fades with washing – worth remembering when you're shopping. If you want Anish Kapoor levels of saturated colour, go for wool, cashmere or silk.

RAINBOW ASS

For men, especially, wearing colour below the waist is a real demonstration of confidence. Choosing trousers in a strong primary will certainly make a statement. Pick well and it can put you,

MORE COLOUR THAN PRIDE, THE CHIC GEEK'S FAVOURITE COLOUR COMBINATIONS – GO BOLD OR GO HOME:

- **RED & GREEN** The colours of the Gucci signature stripe. It's said that the founder, Guccio Gucci, was inspired by the green of the English countryside and the scarlet of British hunting coats.

- **ORANGE & PINK** A confident classic for warmer climates and one popularized by Yves Saint Laurent who – no doubt inspired by his love of Morocco – used it on the label for Rive Gauche. This is BOLD. It shouts 'confidence'.

- **PINK & GREEN** 'Should never be seen' said somebody who didn't know what they were talking about. A personal favourite – known to #FashionWankers as 'prawn cocktail'.

- **BLUE & RED** That's Yves Klein blue and Rothko red: fine art made fashion.

- **PINK & NAVY** Diana Vreeland famously claimed, 'Pink is the navy blue of India.' Why not combine the two?

sartorially, into the David Hockney league as a master of colour. Don't even think about pairing those trousers with a bland shirt, though. Pick something just as bright. Go bold, or go home.

PAN-TONE IT DOWN
Combine different shades of the same colour: red and pink look good together, or try red with another berry colour. Alternatively, go matchy-matchy and make everything the same shade of the same colour. If you get it right, you'll look like a very chic cult member.

STRENGTH IN NUMBERS
Use strong colour in accessories to turn them into sartorial highlights. Think scarves, ties, pocket squares, hats, gloves and shoes. But, if in doubt, less is more when it comes to accessories.

THE CHIC GEEK SAYS

"Don't be afraid of colour. Put strong colour with more strong colour. It's all about balance."

"All colours are friends of their neighbours and the lovers of their opposites."

Marc Chagall

OH FUCK IT, HERE'S A REFRESHER. GETTING COLOURS AND THEIR BEDFELLOWS CORRECT IS SOMETHING WORTH REMINDING YOURSELF OF. HERE'S YOUR #FASHIONWANKERS COLOUR WHEEL CHEAT SHEET TO MAKE EVEN JOSEPH AND HIS TECHNICOLOUR DREAMCOAT LOOK A LITTLE, WELL, PEDESTRIAN.

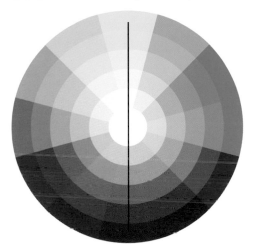

Complementary colours

This is two colours opposite each other on the colour wheel. Because the colours contrast, one stands out while the other accents.

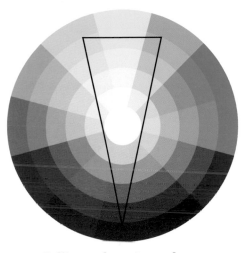

Split-complementary colours

This uses a base colour and two colours adjacent to its complement. Think of it as a softer version of the complementary wheel.

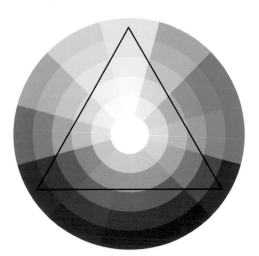

Triadic colours

This is three colours evenly spaced over the wheel. Having three bold colours offers balance.

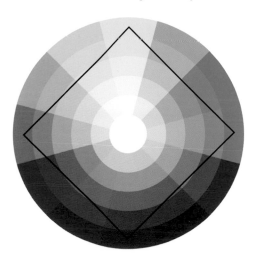

Tetradic colours

This uses two sets of complementary colours. Like the complementary wheel, it's best to let one colour dominate.

SURVIVING
FASHION
WEEK

Linda E was the best supermodel. Fact.

If you love fashion, you'll relish Fashion Week, no matter how above it/over it you think you are. For those who aren't too sure what it even is: it's a bi-annual get together in a specific city during which the fashion community congregates to see new ideas, to take the temperature of the industry and to see where it's going next. As much happens off the catwalk as on it. Here are the answers to all the questions you've ever wanted to ask.

THE CHIC GEEK SAYS...

"Just like cocktail hour, there's a fashion week probably happening, right now, somewhere in the world."

WHERE IN THE WORLD?

The major fashion weeks of the world are New York, London, Milan and Paris and are held in that order.

Paris is the capital of fashion, but London is the world's most fashionable city. New York is more commercial and Milan showcases the best of the Italian brands and their manufacturing industry. There are many other fashion weeks outside these main four, from Seoul to Tokyo to Copenhagen to São Paulo, and, just like cocktail hour, there's a fashion week probably happening somewhere in the world right now.

HOW MANY DAYS IN A 'WEEK'?

We say 'week', but in many cases it's far shorter – but 'Fashion Few Days' wouldn't have quite the same ring. The global circus hits town and everyone gets the chance to watch brands and designers flexing their muscles, both creatively and financially, while aiming to be relevant and influential. It's a lot about the parties, too, and the spectacle of it all.

WHEN DOES IT TAKE PLACE?

Calendar-wise, womenswear fashion weeks are held, roughly, in February and September, while the men have theirs in January and June. The collections are shown a season in advance, so if it's spring, you'll be looking at the forthcoming autumn collection and in autumn, it's the other way round.

Fashion Wanker:
The Floppy-Haired Romantic,
page 97

Standing ticket?
GOODBYE

Fashion brands and designers then take orders for the most popular items or looks (the latter denotes a complete outfit on a model), and spend the following months deciding what to make, making it and delivering it for that season. Although the world of high fashion has flirted with the 'See Now, Buy Now' concept (which would mean that the clothes were available to buy straight after they were shown), the idea has never really worked either commercially or creatively.

HOW LONG DO THE SHOWS LAST?

Fashion shows typically last anywhere from 5 to 20 minutes. The length of any fashion show depends on a couple of factors including the number of looks a designer is showing. Some brands/designers show their men's and women's collections together which often makes the show longer. It's also a reflection of money; the more looks/ models, the more money is being thrown at the show. But if you see a smoke machine and coloured lights, and they're not filming a music video, then you probably need to leave. Stat.

Shows almost invariably run late, although more in some cities than others. London is generally fairly timely, while Milan is delayed Italian time… Just how different each show is from every other is part of their charm. When the lights dim, the music starts and the first model hits the catwalk, even the most jaded Fashion Wanker feels a frisson of excitement at the thought that they just might be about to see the next big thing.

WHO GOES?

Every show is different and brands have different priorities and reasons to invite people. The audience is made up of fashion editors, stylists, bloggers, journalists, buyers, fashion students, interns, influencers, celebrities and friends or employees of the brand. You can request tickets, but the most in demand shows invite according to their list of importance. Some have more celebrities on the front row, while others are more interested in buyers and editors.

WHO SITS WHERE?

The front row – the frow in staccato fashionese – is where the most important buyers/celebrities/media stars are seated. The number it can accommodate varies according to the size of the venue. Most shows seat people on benches so that more can be squeezed in if necessary, although the top shows offer individual seats with namecards on them. If the latter are handwritten, you can start to get excited.

WHAT IS STREET STYLE?

Street style – in fashion week context, anyway – is what's happening outside the shows, with the arrivals and departures of editors, models, influencers and others. The photographers lurking outside each show are snapping content for magazines and social media, noting trends, accessories and outfits with particular attention to anything new, chic, weird or, sometimes, plain outlandish. From their point of view, it's like shooting (very stylish) fish in a barrel. If you want to feature, play it cool and look focused: people to see, places to be. Cheerful apparent indifference is the best catnip for photographers.

Outside the shows is where you'll see the best outfits: it's where fashion becomes real and it's where the next generation of Fashion Wankers come to see and be seen. We were all there once…

How do you SURVIVE? Free champagne for days. Drink your way through it.

HOW TO BLAG
YOUR
WAY
INTO...

The promise of a free bar, a glamorous location and a goodie bag can turn a blagger into a ligger in less time than it takes to shoulder-cape a jacket. If you want to join them there, you need to be confident enough to talk your way in, and comfortable enough when you've succeeded to know that you belong. Fashion shows and parties are a key part of the spectacle of fashion – plus mingling with fun people while knocking back free cocktails and canapés never hurt anybody's Fashion Wanker credibility.

Here are the top tips for bagging your new Fashion Wanker social life.

How to blag your way into a fashion party:

- **TRY THE EASY ROUTE** Google the brand or designer, and see if you can track down the name of the person in charge of PR or at the top of the agency looking after the event. That's the one you'll want to drop in extremis – they won't want to turn you away at the door if you might be, or might know, someone important.

- **DO SOME RESEARCH** Know the time, the location and the reason for the party, and get someone to forward you an invitation if you can. If you can't, see if you can catch a glimpse of an invitation on social media – you should already be following plenty of fashion editors, influencers and so on, and they'll often showcase invitations.

- **RSVP TO THE NOT-FOR-YOU INVITATION** Make sure you copy the 'subject' box from the RSVP e-mail; it will make it look as though you were on the original invitation list. The best result is a positive reply saying that your name is down.

- **MEMORIZE THE NAME OF THE PERSON ON THE INVITATION** If there's a problem on the door, pretend you know them really well.

- **LOOK THE PART** Know the likely dress code for the party and dress accordingly. Looking as though you're meant to be there will help give the impression that you're an asset to the event.

- **DON'T JOIN THE QUEUE** Walk up to the door confidently and don't even glance at the queue. People who are actually invited don't queue. Make eye contact as you speak. Remember buying your first underage drink? This is the mature version.

- **IF YOU'RE TOLD YOUR NAME ISN'T ON THE LIST, SAY "I MESSAGED SO-AND-SO (QUOTE THE NAME YOU CHECKED OUT EARLIER) AND I DEFINITELY RSVP'D"** Facial expression should be mildly concerned but unworried. Don't ever be rude.

- **WHILE IN THE QUEUE SEE IF YOU CAN CATCH A GLIMPSE OF THE LIST** Then just say one of the names you see. Don't say "Anna Wintour" even if you are wearing dark shades.

- **BE A GOOD GUEST** Remember, brands, designers and PRs need bodies to make every event look buzzy and popular. Sometimes you'll be doing them the favour with your good looks and magnetic personality.

- **NEVER PAY FOR A DRINK** Show some self-respect: the minute a bar runs dry or asks you for money, leave.

- **BE REALISTIC** However good your blagging skills, you're not going to get into the Met Gala.

How to blag your way into a fashion show:

- **BE HONEST** Bullshit doesn't always oil the cogs of fashion. Go to the front door, smile and ask nicely. Say, "Hello, would it be possible to come in if there is any available space?" This is more likely to work with smaller fashion designers and brands: they will usually let people in to stand if there is space just before the show is about to start.

- **DON'T GET THERE TOO EARLY** Come to the door looking urgent and hurried. The attitude you're giving out is I've-done-a-gazillion-shows-today-and-I-haven't-got-time-to-be-quizzed.

- **KNOW WHEN TO PUSH AND WHEN TO LEAVE WELL ALONE** If you feel you're speaking to an intern, ask to see somebody more senior. But accept a definite 'no' graciously and politely. Move to the side; there's always next time.

- **KNOW ABOUT SEATING** Fashion weeks often have a single system to denote status and seating, particularly if the show you're going for is at the main designated venue. Look out for the signs: they may be using letters or coloured stickers, for instance. When you've cracked the system, head to the nearest stationers for a Sharpie and the right-coloured dots.

- **NOT THE FRONT ROW** If you've managed to blag your way in, do not sit on the front row. You're not that important, it's the easiest way to be rumbled – and anyway, you're here to see the clothes, not to behave obnoxiously. If the frow isn't full, you'll often be invited to move forward. Then you can make the most of it and hit your social like a Kardashian.

- **WHAT TO DO WHEN THE SHOW'S ABOUT TO BEGIN** If the show is about to start, just get to the back and make sure you can see. When the lights go down, and the music starts, you never know what you're going to see. The excitement of the few short minutes of a show can seem like the most exhilarating in your life.

How to blag free stuff:

- **IF YOU'RE AT A FASHION PARTY OR SHOW** Most events will have a goodie bag. It makes sense to check your coat in, because sometimes the goodie bags are handed out at the coat check. If you spot the stash, make sure that everyone knows when you're leaving: say goodbye to the people standing next to the goodie bags and to everybody else within ear shot. But don't help yourself: it's a #FashionWankers faux pas.

- **IF YOU WANT TO BE SENT FREE STUFF** Start an online platform – blog or Instagram – with a strong identity and voice, and offer to review and feature products. It may take a while for people to notice and respond to what you're doing, but the industry is open to passionate, polite and hardworking people, so if you're doing it right you'll win through in the end.

- **BECOME A FASHION EDITOR** On- or offline. Obviously, this requires a little more work.

- **AND WHEN YOU DO GET GIVEN FREE STUFF** Don't flaunt it. Be modest and don't take anything for granted. Never boast about your haul; it shows a lack of class.

THROW SHADE
WITH STYLE

Throwing shade is the stylish and witty form of insulting others. Remember when the late, great Aretha Franklin dissed Taylor Swift? 'Great gowns, beautiful gowns' was her sole comment on the junior diva. Not bitchy, not snide, but devastating all the same. The Urban Dictionary defines it as 'acting in a casual or disrespectful manner towards someone… dissing a friend.'

This is your chance to be honest and also amusing. It's standard banter among fashion people, so it's worth getting good at. Throwing shade like an Olympian calls for speed, split-second timing and ideally originality. It's the chance to show your creative side in a world where it can be difficult to be critically honest.

"Florals for spring? Groundbreaking"

Miranda Priestly,
The Devil Wears Prada

BASIC SHADE

Here's a few starter lines you could try (or amend to make your own)

"Why are you so obsessed with me?"
= I just wanna know!

"You're not pretty enough to be that dumb"
= Don't be so naïve/obvious

"I wish I could, but I really don't want to"
= Shady way to turn down an invitation

"Green isn't your colour"
= Jealous, much?

HOW TO THROW MORE SHADE THAN RAY-BAN:

Anna Wintour

- Think. Your first thoughts are usually the best, then order them in a way that is funny and cutting. If too much, learn how to edit yourself and lessen the impact. Hitting it bang on is key.
- **Use current references. Your shade is a reflection of how up to date and intelligent you are. Don't leave yourself open for others to think otherwise. Get Googling if you haven't heard of something before.**
- Be critical, but not bitchy. Bitchy is a reflection of you. Don't project.
- **Know your audience and judge how cutting you can afford to be. Don't overdo it if the target is unworthy – nobody wants to be seen kicking a puppy. But, if they want to bring it, then let's go...hold on tight!**
- If you think your shade won't cut the mustard, stay silent.
- **Don't shade people you don't like. It can be read as something else. Your friends will know the shade comes with love.**
- Throw shade online. Have an arsenal of appropriate GIFs ready to fire onto social media for when you're shading remotely, rather than in person.

WHEN SHADE COMES YOUR WAY

- If you're happy to hand it out, you've got to be able to take it.
- **Credit where credit's due – if it's good, it's good. Laugh.**
- If they went low, keep your composure and don't stoop to their level.
- **Timing is all when it comes to your response – don't rush it, but it needs to be pretty rapid.**
- Act nonchalant, as if it doesn't really matter.
- **Respond with the best comeback you can muster.**
- Think. They might have a point.
- **Know when to stop (before everybody stops laughing).**

"Groundbreaking"
= You thought that was original? It's lamely obvious *eyeroll*

"No comment"
= A deafening silence of disgust

"Can I be you for Halloween?"
= Your look is horrifying

RUSHING TO
RELAX

Every so often you'll get the feeling that it's all beginning to be just too much. Focusing on fashion, keeping up with all the other Fashion Wankers, staying on top of your social media and working out which, if any, influencers should be influencing you – along with everything else – can seem relentless. Time for WWGD (WhatWouldGwynethDo)?

TAKE THE MINDFULNESS ROUTE TO KEEP YOURSELF SANE – READ AND ABSORB:

- Don't take everything too seriously. It's fun to keep up with fashion and trends, but at the end of the day none of it really matters (that much).

- **Take a break. Nobody knows everything about fashion and style: we're all learning and evolving. This is part of the fun, but it can also be exhausting.**

- Remember, however competitive it gets, you're playing your own game, not anyone else's – just be the best version of you.

- **Social media isn't real. Those living their best life have bad days too.**

- Don't get into debt for fashion. You'll survive without it.

- **Stop and enjoy the moment. You look hot. Smile.**

- And, remember, if things ever get too much, dial #FashionWankers Anonymous – 0800-I-AM-A-WANKER

 thanks Gwynnie

"Know first
who you are,
and then
adorn yourself
accordingly"

Epictetus

ULTIMATE FASHION
WANKERS

The most stylish people EVER! This is the pinnacle, the top, the apex, the climax, the summit of the Everest of style. These people exude style from their little fingers and are the gods of our crazy Fashion Wankers world.

We look to these people, with their images stuck forever in our consciousness, for their elegance, quirkiness and balls. These are the people who aren't afraid to push the boundaries and have that innate ability to make it work for them. Welcome to the Fashion Wankers Hall of Fame (FWHOF).

OTHERS:

James Dean
Charles Rennie
Mackintosh
Samuel-Jean Pozzi
David Bowie
Jimi Hendrix
Magenta Devine
Princess Diana
Bobby Moore

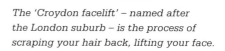

Model Wanker: Kate Moss

The 'Croydon facelift' – named after the London suburb – is the process of scraping your hair back, lifting your face.

Kate Moss From the Croydon facelift to the Highgate high-life, this girl is cool personified.

Marlon Brando The bad-boy-biker in a classic white tee and leather jacket oozes timeless masculinity.

Elizabeth Taylor This beauty queen collected husbands like jewellery and never lost her sparkle.

Paul Newman An example of a man who never overcomplicated his look. But, then again, why would you when you look this handsome?

Marilyn Monroe While Monroe only wore five drops of Chanel No. 5 and nothing else in bed, her style was all about flaunting those sultry curves.

Alain Delon This French film star is pure Gallic nonchalance, whether in a slim-cut suit or skimpy St Tropez swimwear.

Steve McQueen The definition of dressed-down menswear, McQueen could make the boring look cool.

George Best This enigmatic Irishman pioneered the footballer as pin-up and became a style icon.

Cleopatra Okay, so we're still thinking Elizabeth Taylor, but you just know this Egyptian queen was owning the BC world.

Bad-boy Wanker: **Marlon Brando**

Iconic Wanker: **Elizabeth Taylor**

Cool Hand Wanker: **Paul Newman**

Blonde Bombshell Wanker: **Marilyn Monroe**

Nonchalant Wanker: **Alain Delon**

Dressed-down Wanker: **Steve McQueen**

Football Wanker: **George Best**

Queen Wanker: **Cleopatra**

"I don't do fashion, I am fashion"
Coco Chanel

REPEAT AFTER ME: THINGS FASHION WANKERS SAY

The things Fashion Wankers say change all the time, so the definitions here are fluid: there's no room for rigidity when it comes to expressing yourself.

"EW" When you find something disgusting.

"I'M DONE" You're mentally walking away.

"CRINGE" When something is embarrassingly bad or awkward

"NEXT!" When you're over something. Happens quickly in this game.

"YAS, QWEEN" An enthusiastic and supportive endorsement – thumbs up.

"WHO ARE YOU WEARING?" Are you dressed up or not?

"CHANNELLING _____" Insert somebody cool, stylish or otherwise aspirational.

"REALNESS" Realistically passing for something or someone else.

"DEAD" (also used: I DIE) When something is so good it's the best.

"OUCH" When somebody's shade or critic goes straight to target.

"OBSESSED" You're SO into it.

"NO FUCKS GIVEN" An emphatic form of saying you don't care.

"FUCKS GIVEN" A reverse form of saying you care.

"BORING" Something no-one wants to be described as. Even bad is better than boring.

THINGS FASHION WANKERS
NEVER SAY

In our visual world, words are still just as important as images. A signifier of your style intelligence and know-how, using the wrong words at the wrong time will make you stick out like a sore thumb (like a Minimalist Wanker at a Gucci show).

Be honest and, for god's sake, have an opinion. As you get more experienced in Fashion Wanker surroundings, your internal database starts to fill with references. Read, watch and try everything at least once – it'll give you the context, the background into which everything fits. But knowing what *not* to say is a part of it too.

Just like stupid people who think they're clever – sophomania – wannabe Fashion Wankers get caught out with too many of the wrong phrases.

PHRASES TO AVOID

"Fashion emergency" Everyone knows that nothing (in) fashion is that important. **"I'm on the list"** You're clearly not. **"Directional"** Best left to the SatNav. **"Iconic"** It's not iconic if it's forgotten in a year. **"Pièce de résistance"** Non. Non. Non. Smacks of conscious sophistication. **"Dapper"** Usually associated with men in skinny three-piece suits – don't use it unless you think a pocket square is cool. **"Google me"** No. Best not to tempt fate. **"Everything"** You're guaranteed to be an over-user of this. **"Funky"** Get back to the 60s. **"That's neat"** Leave it to Kevin Costner unintentionally dissing Madonna in *Truth or Dare*. **"I'm so lucky, I'm sample size"** Humble-bragging at its worst. Get in the sea. **"No brown in town"** It's not 1934 anymore. **"Spenny"** 'Expensive' is fine. **"It was gifted"** It really wasn't. Just admit that you paid full price for it. **"I'm a big fan of Philipp Plein"** Will sound alarm bells. **"I only drink champagne"** #FashionWankers love anything sparkling, as long as it's free. **"(Insert name here) is the new Alexander McQueen" As if. **"Groundbreaking"** Don't say this if you mean it. **"Interesting"** This only tells people you don't know what you just saw. HAVE AN OPINION. **"I'd like to show more he-vage"** Guys, put your tits away. **"I'd love to have gone to the <major designer> party, but it clashed with <whatever>"** Sure, hun. You were NFI. **"It's vintage"** It's not vintage if it's 5-years-old and from Primark. **"I got it in a sample sale"** Everyone, you included, knows that that particular designer/brand never has sample sales, or discounts anything. **"Dolce & Gabbana have such depth"** Very dangerous ground. **"Absolutely flawless"** Unless you're talking about a really big diamond. **"It's couture"** Don't use unless the garment in question was handmade in Paris and you had to get a second mortgage to buy it.

Luxury Tries to denote something better and exclusive, but is lazily applied to everything these days. **Sustainable** Often used to 'greenwash' fashion – and often far from true. **Natural** Meaning what, exactly? Isn't everything found on Earth 'natural'? **Modern** Wildly overused – try 'contemporary' instead. **Nice** Feeble – and sounds like a backhanded compliment. **Timeless** Nothing is 'timeless', everything will date, although plenty of things date in a good way.

DANDIER THAN A DANDELION

Chanel handbag

FAKES &
FADDERS

It's a classic game of Fashion Wanker jeopardy:
you scale the giddy heights of the fads while
trying to avoid the fakes. It's not down to the roll
of the dice: you're the one in control.

SPOT THE FAKES

- You can fake it until you make it. The key to reaching the nirvana of Fashion Wanker greatness is confidence, competence and an optimistic outlook. Just between you and I, we're all fakers hoping to make it, we're just at differing stages.

- **It's an attitude, a confidence. Knowing who you are, where you are and why you're there.**

- Do your research. Know your shit or know you're shit. (*See* How To Blag Your Way Into... on page 48).

- **It takes a real Fashion Wanker to spot other Fashion Wankers – cool for cool. This is the crowd you're trying to impress. It's also important to recognize one another and let them know by paying them a compliment. Don't be afraid to say hello.**

- Seek advice. If you like something on somebody else, don't be afraid to ask, where did you get that from?

- **The point is not to be popular, it is to be good.**

- Always ask; Über Stylist or Uber driver?

- **The whole ruse of being a true Fashion Wanker means you never quite make it. You're always striving to improve, keep up and show another facet of your style or personality and that's what keeps fashion rolling on. It's the journey we're all on. Enjoy the ride.**

FAD IT

- Fads, trends or crazes are when a group of people do or wear the same things at the same time. The best #FashionWankers lead or are the first to pick up on these and take the risk by sticking their necks out on something new.

- **The fashion industry likes fads and trends because it makes us buy more.**

- Fads are the types of things that make us do things, that when we look back, we think, "what the hell was I thinking?". Thank god for photography!

- **They can come from anywhere and involve anything. Knowing which to ignore and which to take on board is the key to looking good. It's important to know what suits you. It's also important knowing when to let a fad go and stop wearing something. It's knowing when it's time to bin those skinny jeans.**

- Sometimes it's good to roll your sleeves up and just get involved. Don't over think it. They can also creep up on you.

- **The trick is to ace the fad. Make it your own and take it up a notch. It'll probably take you onto the next one. Once you're ahead, you stay ahead.**

- Fads fade, usually, when the novelty has gone. (Sad face).

THE CHIC GEEK SAYS...

"Mutton or lamb? You'll only be mutton if you're trying to look younger."

Something of an urban fashion myth, the Dropper (AKA the Flipper) manages to make a profit from selling already overpriced clothes and other fashion items at even more inflated prices. The prices escalate due to scarcity and demand, or so the story goes.

Who needs a Saturday job flipping burgers when you can make handsome pocket money flipping designer sneakers? In China they call it 'Daigou' (dye-go), or 'to buy on behalf', and it describes the practice of purchasing sought-after goods with the goal of selling them on. Sometimes the profit comes from price arbitrage, sometimes it really is due to the item's scarcity, but the Dropper knows that it's all about timing. 'Product drops' – what most of us would call deliveries – create the hype for limited-edition products to sell on, and the Dropper has figured out when and where and will be first in line to get the goods that everyone else will want but be just a bit too late to buy from source. The Dropper will then exploit the thwarted shoppers to create a frenzied bidding war and make a handsome return on the stylish investments. Sneakers and watches are the products which reap the best returns.

BRANDS

Supreme
Palace
End Clothing
Rolex
Patek Philippe
Nike
Foot Locker

COLOURS

Queue camouflage:
something nondescript
that you won't be noticed in.

ICONIC ITEM

Vacheron Constantin 57260

Flipper
Flipper
Flipper
Flipper
Flipper
Flipper
Flipper

"I like my money right where I can see it . . . hanging in my closet"

Carrie Bradshaw, *Sex & the City*

HOW TO SMASH YOUR SOCIAL MEDIA
LIKE AN AVOCADO

You can turn your router off, of course, but other ways to break the internet are unpredictable.
You may hear of ways of 'disrupting' or 'amplifying' stuff, but they're mostly bullshit concocted by digital marketeers. Who needs real friends when you have a social media life? It's all the validation we need, isn't it? But, seriously, there are a few things you can do that will increase your social (media) life and make you more digitally popular.

THE CHIC GEEK SAYS...

"Who needs masses of followers anyway? I love you for all your fashion-wankiness!"

"Remind yourself.
Nobody's built like you,
you design yourself"

JAY-Z

- **Start a pod. First find some friends or, at the very least, people who are as bothered about social media as you are. Then start a WhatsApp group and message everyone the moment after you upload your content. The more comments you recieve the more likely it is that the algorithm will prioritize you and your content will be pushed out to more people.**

- Be original. If the idea or concept is good or funny, then it has a bigger chance of 'going viral'. It needs to connect with people. Social media is unpredictable, especially if you're not famous, but who knows what will happen and that's part of the unpredictability.

- **Be regular and consistent. You can't post once and expect something huge to happen.**

- Show your face. Faces get an average of 38% more 'likes' than photos without.

- **Get one of the Kardashians to like your posts. If you're not friends with one of them, take the lesser option and ask your most-followed friends to like your content.**

- Remember, social media companies are always only interested in their own success and business. Be prepared to adapt to survive.

- **Tag people in to draw attention to your posts. But don't become a social media nag.**

- Remember to use hashtags to up the chance of people finding you. (And use #FashionWankers at all times when you're looking your finest…)

- **Negative posts often go further, but unless you're desperately thirsty for attention, try to stay positive. Negativity often breeds negativity.**

- If you're feeling burnt out, take a break. Even delete it. It's okay.

- **Follow@thechicgeekcouk & make sure you use the hashtag #FashionWankers. I want to see who you're wearing.**

HOW TO BE AN
INFLUENCER

'Influencers' think they have more reach than S Club 7 and more engagement than Elizabeth Taylor – or so they like to tell you. Always on, these young Wankers judge others solely by the numbers of followers they have and how perfect their life looks through a lens. Who needs reality when it's this exhausting being photogenic? They just shot a 'campaign' in the bathroom, btw.

HOW TO LIVE YOUR BEST LIFE AS AN INFLUENCER:

- Get busy snapping. Influencers have more perfect images than hot dinners. They're too busy taking pictures of the food to eat anyway.

- **Be original. Have an individual identity both in terms of look and attitude.**

- Accesorize your life. Use props like balloons, flowers, cakes and tiled floors.

- **You no longer take holidays. To an Influencer, every destination is now a photo opportunity.**

- Colour is your best friend. Grab people's eye and attention.

- **Work hard. Research and plan. Be a leader.**

- Add some reality (without a filter). Perfect is boring all of the time.

- **Don't sweat it. We'll look back in a few years, when Instagram is long gone and something new has replaced it, and think 'What was all the fuss about?'**

- And if all else fails, make yourself a papier-mache head in your own image (Like The Chic Geek!).

THE CHIC GEEK SAYS...

"What happened to Narcissus when he fell into the pool of water? It doesn't matter as long as somebody got the perfect shot!"

GODS

Kylie Jenner
Justin Bieber
Ariana Grande
Chiara Ferragni
Zoella
Pelayo Diaz
Eva Chen
Frida Kahlo

COLOURS

Anything that ties in with the background-of-the-moment, whether it's Brooklyn's stepped brownstones or pastel houses in Notting Hill.

ICONIC ITEM

A monogrammed phone case

Frida Kahlo

THE FASHION WANKER
10 COMMANDMENTS

THOU SHALL
**Be grateful for what you have.
There's only one of you. You're unique.**

THOU SHALL NOT
**Be wasteful.
Be responsible about taking only
what you need.**

THOU SHALL
Educate thyself. Learn through experience.

THOU SHALL NOT
Murder fashion.

THOU SHALL
**Dress fashionably.
But not every trend is for everyone.**

When Moses came back from Mount Sinai with the Ten Commandments, who was he wearing? The Chic Geek can go one better with a simple list of the do's and don'ts of achieving and maintaining your Fashion Wanker status. Here are the Fashion Wanker commandments to religiously stick to:

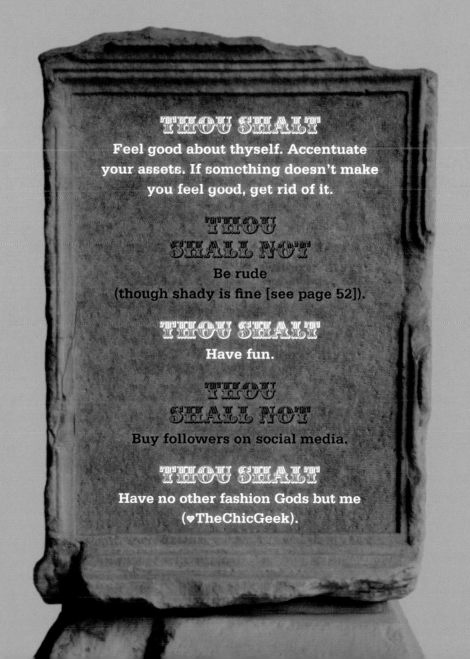

THOU SHALT
Feel good about thyself. Accentuate your assets. If something doesn't make you feel good, get rid of it.

THOU SHALL NOT
Be rude
(though shady is fine [see page 52]).

THOU SHALT
Have fun.

THOU SHALL NOT
Buy followers on social media.

THOU SHALT
Have no other fashion Gods but me
(♥TheChicGeek).

TOTALLY WOULD

Possessing charisma and sex appeal, as well as a stonking sense of style, is a rare combination. It's a triple thirsty threat and it's what makes this group of individuals very special.

This is more than a celebrity crush, or a phwoah (heart) on Instagram, this is an I-wanna-rip-your-clothes-off-but-first-I-need-to-appreciate-the-outfit type mentality. These Fashion Wankers have it all and their sense of style just adds to their attractiveness.

Harry Styles Is he, isn't he? Who cares? Everybody wants him, in all directions! **David Beckham** More hairstyles than Supercuts, Beckham likes to play with how he looks and nearly always pulls it off. White budgie smugglers included. **Mick Jagger** Always wearing something he can move in, or so the song goes, early Jagger puts sexual energy into style. **Tilda Swinton** Androgynous goddess, Swinton is one of the world's greatest clothes horses. **Jude Law** He has that laissez-faire attitude of cheeky dishevelment. Hey, Jude. **Cate Blanchett** She makes difficult clothes look easy and that's the sign of somebody who has major inner style. **J-Lo** The banging body is covered in just enough while still keeping it classy. A difficult balance. **Prince Albert** The Prince Consort had a magnetic elegance even if he's now mostly remembered for being the name of a certain intimate piercing. **Lenny Kravitz** Rock 'n' roll sexiness, Kravitz's style is as cool as his cucumber. (Google that). **Tom Ford** From the dance floor of Studio 54 to reinventing some of the biggest fashion brands in the world, Ford is 'Fucking Fabulous'. **Tom Selleck** That 'tache. Selleck sex appeal emerges every summer along with his hibiscus-patterned Hawaiian shirt.

Hawaii Wanker: **Tom Selleck**, 1980

THE FUTURE OF
FASHION

Fashion always has one eye on the future. As a global business, its objective is simply to sell more – and more – stuff. But there's a revolution due: the ways in which we consume fashion and look at how to lessen its impact on the environment will increasingly influence how we look in the next few years. If you're wondering how, here are The Chic Geek's top five future fashion predictions. (Remember, you read them here first):

AI TAKEOVER

Every time we shop, we're buying somebody's taste and ideas. And, given that we're used to a choice of literally thousands of options, we won't want that to stop. In the future, when sewbots are manufacturing most of our clothes, we'll be able to customize beyond the wildest dreams of even the fussiest #FashionWankers. Using 3D printers, you'll be able to print out and wear your own products, customizing them perfectly in terms of fit, cut and finish. It will also be the death of sales (sadly) because retailers will no longer have to second guess the consumer and make products months in advance to then be discounted when they don't sell. All of this can be delivered by automated vehicles at low cost, conveniently and quickly.

SPOTIFASHION

What's the largest thing in your bedroom after your bed? It's probably your closet. How much of what's in it do you wear regularly? If you have a lot of clothes, it's probably a small percentage. But you don't need to own, wash, iron and store this stuff – it takes up valuable space in your head as well as your wardrobe. For #FashionWankers, washing and ironing clothes feels like a trip back to the Victorian age, with processes designed to waste your valuable leisure time.

In the future, you won't own the majority of your clothes. Of course, you'll have your own underwear and a few personal things, but everything else will be serviced and supplied by others. An office worker who wants 5 work shirts for Monday morning will place an order online, have them delivered and then, once worn, collected again on Friday. At the end of their lives, the shirts will be recycled. The Spotifying of functional, day-to-day clothes will free up time and space for consumers. Plus you'll have unlimited opportunities to express yourself in different ways by means of affordable subscriptions.

SMARTCLOTHES

Fashion is going to get clever. Beyond fashion or cut, your smartclothes are going to start multitasking – they won't waste the hours they spend on your back: they'll be recharging your phone or assessing your carb intake or monitoring your health. New fabric technology could even see your clothes cleaning the polluted air around you. Rather than looking back to styles and functions that haven't really changed for centuries, the form of your clothes will start to be dictated by the jobs they have to do – and that's going to change how you look, too.

GET OFF MY SCRAPHEAP

What happens to all the stuff you don't want? You can't just keep sending it to charity shops or giving it away, hoping it gets a second life somewhere a long way away. It doesn't. There are just too many clothes in the world now and it's becoming a big problem. We need to reuse and recycle – and this means looking at clothes like the other things you dispose of and taking them back to raw materials. At the moment, this is expensive but, as the process becomes quicker and cheaper, you'll start to recycle clothes as you do glass or paper. Virgin materials (and the environmental burden they carry) will become a thing of the past: you'll be wearing new things made from the fibres of old things.

ACKNOWLEDGE DISPOSABILITY

Like everyone else, you say you care about the environment, but when it comes to stumping up more cash, do you walk the talk? In the future you'll acknowledge and accept your desire for constant novelty and things will be manufactured that can be binned easily, cheaply – and without putting a burden on your conscience. The white paper shirt (once a 1960s novelty) will return as an everyday reality: once worn, it can go straight to recycling. Enjoy!

The future's bright, the future's #FashionWankers

FASHION WANKER BINGO

HOW TO PLAY
FASHION WANKER
BINGO

This is bingo, but not like a game of bingo you've ever played before. The rules, if you've participated in the past, remain the same, but with a Fashion Wanker twist. On the following pages you will find all the components you need to play Fashion Wanker Bingo.

This is a game for up to 8 Fashion Wankers to enjoy.

INCLUDED IS

- 8 reversable bingo cards (total of 16 different cards)
- 72 balls
- 36 markers

HOW TO PLAY

Each player chooses a bingo card. Rather than numbers, each bingo card features a recognizable Fashion Wanker dressed in an outfit of five items.

One player is selected as the caller. Their job is to choose 'balls' at random. Likewise, rather than displaying numbers, each of these 'balls' describes an item of clothing.

The game starts when everyone has a card and the caller then picks the first 'ball'. If you have it, you mark it off with a marker. If you don't, you can't. And the caller continues. Once you've collected all the items of clothing to dress your Fashion Wanker, shout 'Fashion Wanker!' to win.

The first to have their outfit complete is the winner.

Bingo cards

Bingo 'balls'

Markers

THE MAGPIE

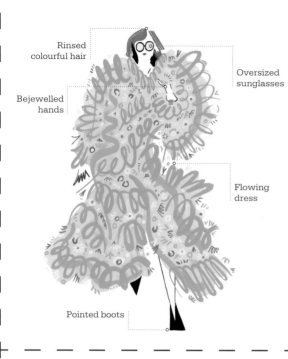

Rinsed colourful hair

Oversized sunglasses

Bejewelled hands

Flowing dress

Pointed boots

THE PARISIAN X-RAY

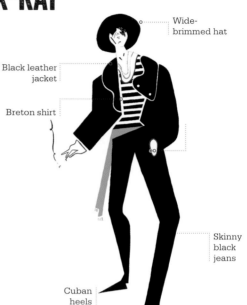

Wide-brimmed hat

Black leather jacket

Breton shirt

Skinny black jeans

Cuban heels

THE METROPOLITAN ELITE

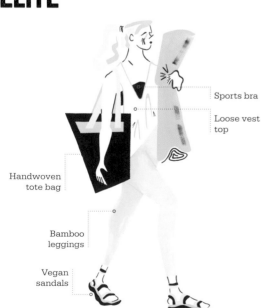

Sports bra

Loose vest top

Handwoven tote bag

Bamboo leggings

Vegan sandals

THE SNEAKER GEEK

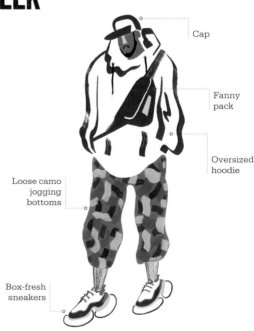

Cap

Fanny pack

Oversized hoodie

Loose camo jogging bottoms

Box-fresh sneakers

THE KNOW-IT-ALL

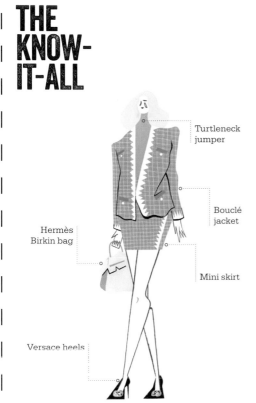

Turtleneck jumper

Bouclé jacket

Hermès Birkin bag

Mini skirt

Versace heels

THE MINI-MALIST

Cashmere beanie

Plain coat, oversized

Plain white T-shirt

Slim Nudie jeans

Chelsea boots

THE ARCHIVIST

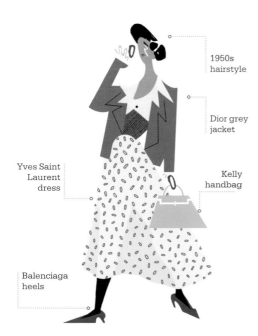

1950s hairstyle

Dior grey jacket

Yves Saint Laurent dress

Kelly handbag

Balenciaga heels

THE VINTAGE DEVOTEE

Twiddly facial hair

Waistcoat

Tweed jacket

Plus fours

Brogues

SCORECARD
FASHION WANKER
BINGO

Player 1	Player 2	Player 3	Player 4	Player 5	Player 6	Player 7	Player 8

SPOT
THE
FAS
WA

HION
NKER

SPOT THE
FASHION WANKER

There are as many Fashion Wankers as fashion lovers out there, so this section is a who's who of some of the key tribes and types: a snapshot of the current fashion landscape. And you're bound to spot plenty of characteristics that you and your friends have in common with some of them...

This collection of characters is just the tip of the Fashion Wankers iceberg, though – there are plenty of crossovers, a morphing of one into the other, and others that have only just been invented, or are about to be.

None of us Fashion Wankers can be rigidly pigeonholed, since the one constant is change – whichever kind you are (or aspire to be), you've probably also got a chameleon-like capacity to adjust to your surroundings.

Choosing your inner Fashion Wanker is about being yourself: it's deep, it's shallow, it's Wanky, it's whatever you want it to be. If the Blahnik fits…

Remember. Being a Fashion Wanker is something to be proud of. Even if you think you're more Romford than Tom Ford, there's a Fashion Wanker in all of us, and it's always time to let him or her out.

Which wanker are you? Shut the front Dior!

SPOT THE WANKER:
THE KNOW-IT-ALL

On a diet of Diet Prada, the Know-It-All knows everything when it comes to fashion, or famous people wearing fashion, or designers designing fashion or anything else that you didn't realize you needed to know.

She's seen it all, she's got the T-shirt, indeed she saw the graduate collection which, by the way, had already been done by so-and-so in spring '96, whose influence was…. You get the idea.

Since nothing is new, she tends to stick to the fashion classics to be on the safe side. To paraphrase Shania, it's a you-don't-impressa-me-much look at fashion, in which she's determined to stay blasé whatever the provocation. Along the way she sucks the life out of the new and the interesting, patrolling social media like a one-woman hit squad, ever-ready to correct her browbeaten audience on the minutiae of fashion and its creators.

CHECKLIST

LOCATION:

DATE:

DESCRIPTION:

OVERHEARD:

ACCESSORIES:

ADDICTED TO Facts.

BRANDS The newest, the most obscure, the up-and-coming ones nobody else has ever heard of.

MANTRA/MOTTO I went to their graduate show.

WHAT NOT TO SAY TO THEM That designer you raved about? I just made them up.

GODS Yves Saint Laurent; Coco Chanel; John Galliano; Anna Wintour; Christian Dior; Cristóbal Balenciaga; Alexander McQueen.

ICONIC ITEM Chanel 2.55 bag.

COLOURS Beige.

TEXTILES Silk and lambskin.

ACCESSORIES Manolo Blahnik's Hangisi court shoes; Gucci snaffle loafers; Hermès Birkin bag; Hermès H Belt.

WANKER RATING

/ 10

THE KNOW-IT-ALL

The Know-It-All is a contrarian, too, always disagreeing with your opinion and making you feel stupid for not knowing something obscure. "I've heard of Fashion Wankers – already out of date" she'll eyeroll. Get a life. This bouji babe loves the safety of her luxe labels. On Wednesdays she wears pink.

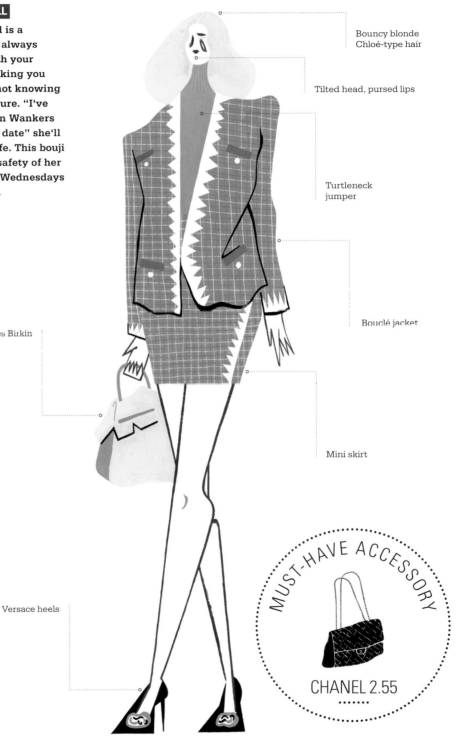

Bouncy blonde Chloé-type hair

Tilted head, pursed lips

Turtleneck jumper

Bouclé jacket

Hermès Birkin

Mini skirt

Versace heels

MUST-HAVE ACCESSORY

CHANEL 2.55

THE MINI- MALIST

CHECKLIST

LOCATION:

DATE:

DESCRIPTION:

OVERHEARD:

ACCESSORIES:

Keeping things very simple, the Minimalist is devoted to clean lines and a monochrome palette. He's been perfecting Scandi style since it wasn't invented. He's safe, boring and perfectly content with the status quo: a visual vacuum.

His wardrobe is stripped back to a simplicity which fits together as seamlessly as a Lego set. Plus he's OCD about order: everything has its place and that's where it should stay.

He has his own podcast that nobody listens to and his own brand – Navajo – of scented white candles. Really?

He's always on the hunt for the perfect trouser or T-shirt, even though he already owns about 50 white ones, all organic FYI. He's repelled by colour and pattern. Off-white? That's a shade to him, not a brand.

ADDICTED TO Nothing.

BRANDS Acne; Neil Barrett; Jil Sander; Helmut Lang; Maison Martin; Margiela; Veja; Nudie Jeans; COS; The Row; Muji.

MANTRA/MOTTO Less is more.

WHAT NOT TO SAY TO THEM Boring!

GODS Jonny Johansson; Donald Judd; Frank Stella; Carl Andre; Helmut Lang; Le Corbusier.

ICONIC ITEM The perfect white T-shirt.

COLOURS White (and black).

TEXTILES Organic cotton.

ACCESSORIES Minimal watch; plain black rucksack; ribbed cashmere beanie; Veja organic canvas sneakers.

WANKER RATING

/ 10

THE MINIMALIST

Style-wise, the Minimalist is a blank sheet. The most radical thing he's introduced to his look in the last decade is the French tuck. Gasp.

Cashmere beanie

Plain coat, oversized

Plain white T-shirt

Slim Nudie jeans

Chelsea boots

MUST-HAVE ACCESSORY

RIBBED BEANIE

SPOT THE WANKER:
THE ARCHIVIST

The Archivist or fashion collector is a curious Wanker. She knows the complete back catalogue of Raf Simons and can actually name all six designers in the Antwerp Six. The Archivist sucks the life out of their love of fashion, or their particular 'oeuvre', by not actually wearing the stuff. Please, don't touch!

She focuses on the big three: Yves Saint Laurent, John Galliano and Alexander McQueen. When she's not busy cataloging – sorry, archiving – or lending it out to exhibitions, she's trawling the sale rooms or eBay for that fabled, unlabelled couture Balenciaga.

For her male equivalent, or at least the one who specializes in menswear, what's desirable is seriously technical and sporty. The more pockets the better. Antique military and workwear are the targets, and anything worn in action is a must.

CHECKLIST

LOCATION:

DATE:

DESCRIPTION:

OVERHEARD:

ACCESSORIES:

WANKER RATING

/ 10

ADDICTED TO BNWT (Brand New With Tags).

BRANDS Raf Simons; Comme des Garçons; C.P. Company; Mary Katrantzou; Alexander McQueen.

MANTRA/MOTTO It's an archive, not a collection.

WHAT NOT TO SAY TO THEM Does the date really matter?

GODS Raf Simons; Helmut Lang; Vivienne Westwood; Massimo Osti; Daphne Guinness; Isabella Blow; Azzedine Alaïa.

ICONIC ITEM The lipstick-print skirt, Prada (the original from 2000).

COLOURS Dior grey.

TEXTILES The latest high-tech materials or those handwoven on the oldest looms.

ACCESSORIES Original Kelly bag.

THE ARCHIVIST

The Archivist's closet space makes Imelda Marcos look like an amateur, and she'll sacrifice anything for that one-off piece of hand-embroidered 1950s French couture. Nothing need actually be in her size. What does she actually wear? You'd never notice.

1950s hairstyle

Dior grey jacket

Yves Saint Laurent dress

Kelly handbag

Balenciaga heels

MUST-HAVE ACCESSORY

KELLY BAG

SPOT THE WANKER:
THE VINTAGE DEVOTEE

Nothing is new. Nothing. This nostalgist sees glamour only in the past – he positively embraces the escapist qualities of dressing in a time when fabrics were scratchy and cufflinks a necessity. He's gazing back to an era when people had manners and the world spun at a slower pace. He and his kind are time-warp reminders of the care and attention people used to take over their appearance.

Always 'dressed', the Vintage Devotee's key calendar event is the Goodwood Revival, where his look becomes the norm and he finds himself in his natural habitat, strolling amongst the old signs and vintage cars.

When he's not dancing a virtuoso jitterbug with a thrilled partner, he's rummaging and trawling through rails at vintage fairs, then mothballing and shoe-treeing his finds in his antique mahogany wardrobe.

CHECKLIST

LOCATION:

DATE:

DESCRIPTION:

OVERHEARD:

ACCESSORIES:

WANKER RATING

/ 10

ADDICTED TO A bargain.

BRANDS Nothing less than two decades old. Preferably five decades or more.

MANTRA/MOTTO Modern life is rubbish.

WHAT NOT TO SAY TO THEM Is that Ralph Lauren?

GODS Katherine Hepburn; Ossie Clark; Gustav Temple; Christina Hendricks; Celia Birtwell; Gene Kelly; Betty Boop; Jarvis Cocker.

ICONIC ITEM Tweed jacket.

COLOURS Earthy.

TEXTILES Itchy.

ACCESSORIES For Him: patterned cravat; trilby. For Her: crocodile handbag, well polished; fur tippet; headscarf.

THE VINTAGE DEVOTEE

This wanker has an allergic reaction to fast fashion – make do and mend is his mantra. Dress for victory!

Twiddly facial hair

Quirky tie

Waistcoat

Pocket square

Tweed jacket

Plus fours

Brogues

MUST-HAVE ACCESSORY

CROCODILE BAG

SPOT THE WANKER:
THE BASIC

He's probably still wearing slashed skinny jeans with a long-line T-shirt full of Yeezy holes because the Basic likes to keep it, well, basic. In his head, though, it's a 'look'. When not at the gym or going through his arduous Patrick Bateman-level grooming routine, he always remembers to cast a long, lingering look back over his shoulder, even when he's just crossing the road (if you missed it, don't worry – it's been recorded for posterity on Instagram).

Basic bros and bitches holiday in Dubai and 'Vegas', and drink iced coffee at Costa or Starbucks. Though he thinks he's individual, he looks the same as all other Basics and tends to move in a pack – and he likes it like that.

He uses Instagram as a personal photo album and he rates others first and foremost on their looks.

CHECKLIST

LOCATION:

DATE:

DESCRIPTION:

OVERHEARD:

ACCESSORIES:

ADDICTED TO Fortnite and skinny jeans.

BRANDS SikSilk; Nike; Louis Vuitton; Reebok; Michael Kors; Ugg; Diesel; Nicce.

MANTRA/MOTTO Blame the game, not the player.

WHAT NOT TO SAY TO THEM Feeling cute, might delete later?

GODS Taylor Swift; Kim Kardashian; Cristiano Ronaldo; Paris Hilton; Zac Efron; Tom Daley.

ICONIC ITEM Distressed denim jeans.

COLOURS Light washes.

TEXTILES Denim and jersey.

ACCESSORIES For Both: shark's tooth necklace; Ray-Ban Wayfarers; Ugg boots. For Her: Michael Kors handbag.

WANKER RATING

/ 10

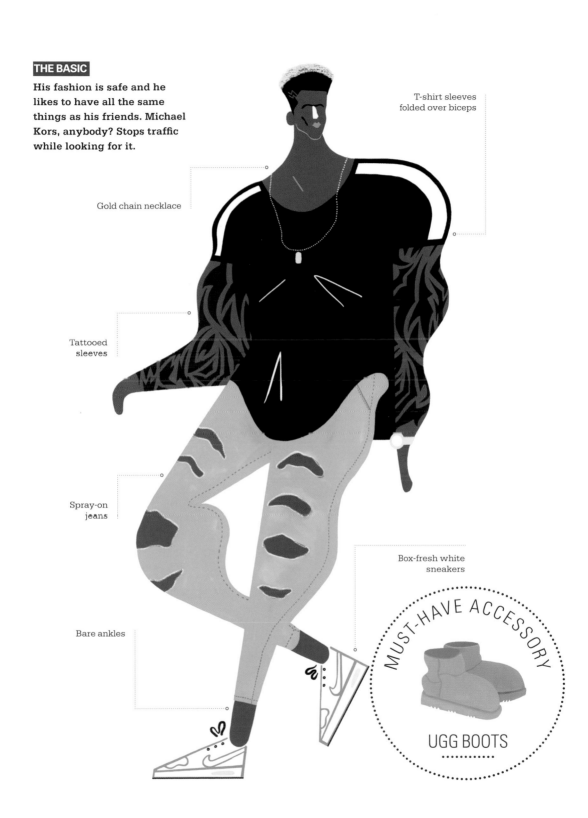

THE BASIC

His fashion is safe and he likes to have all the same things as his friends. Michael Kors, anybody? Stops traffic while looking for it.

Gold chain necklace

T-shirt sleeves folded over biceps

Tattooed sleeves

Spray-on jeans

Box-fresh white sneakers

Bare ankles

MUST-HAVE ACCESSORY

UGG BOOTS

SPOT THE WANKER:
THE FLOPPY-HAIRED ROMANTIC

Who said romance was dead? This polysexual pin-up has put out that he likes guys and girls but is never seen up close and personal with either. Perhaps it's because it's inherently lonely being quite this attractive...

Not since the age of Lord Byron has the world been so obsessed with Floppy-Haired Romantics – the tousled hair and the ambiguous sexuality has a magnetic attraction for everyone.

An artist and thinking person's crush, this is a wanker channelling the lounge lizards of the 20th century with all the sex appeal and charisma oozing under the cover of cherubic innocence. Never been kissed, or have they? It's the question mark and intrigue that keeps the focus squarely on this flamboyant group of Floppy-Haired Romantics.

CHECKLIST

LOCATION:

DATE:

DESCRIPTION:

OVERHEARD:

ACCESSORIES:

WANKER RATING

/ 10

ADDICTED TO Florals.

BRANDS Gucci; Edward Sexton; Loewe; JW Anderson; Liberty of London; Antony Price; Mr. Fish.

MANTRA/MOTTO Call me by your name.

WHAT NOT TO SAY TO THEM Number one all over?

GODS Timothée Chalamet; Harry Styles; Alessandro Michele; Lana Del Rey; Jared Leto; Mick Jagger (youthful version); Kit Harrington.

ICONIC ITEM Anything that shows off those snake hips.

COLOURS Makes a peacock look mundane.

TEXTILES Printed silk and lurex.

ACCESSORIES Pinky ring; multiple delicate necklaces; thin fringed scarf; pointed Beatle boots.

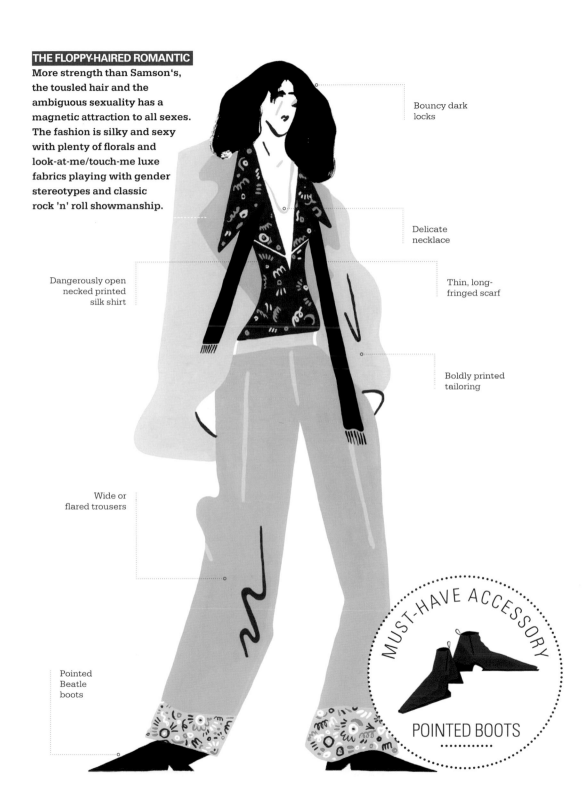

THE FLOPPY-HAIRED ROMANTIC

More strength than Samson's, the tousled hair and the ambiguous sexuality has a magnetic attraction to all sexes. The fashion is silky and sexy with plenty of florals and look-at-me/touch-me luxe fabrics playing with gender stereotypes and classic rock 'n' roll showmanship.

Bouncy dark locks

Delicate necklace

Dangerously open necked printed silk shirt

Thin, long-fringed scarf

Boldly printed tailoring

Wide or flared trousers

Pointed Beatle boots

MUST-HAVE ACCESSORY

POINTED BOOTS

SPOT THE WANKER:
THE GYM BUNNY

The Gym Bunny doesn't spend all those hours weighing out chicken on a Sunday night and freezing in ice baths just for herself, you know. There wouldn't be much point if she didn't record herself and her bodily achievements on social media. Queen of the shameless selfie, including the belfie (butt selfie), the drelfie (drunk selfie) and the shelfie (as you'd guess – and groaning with beauty and grooming products), the Gym Bunny also always knows which of the gym mirrors has the best lighting.

When not selfieing, the Gym Bunny is worrying about her next perfect ponytail and working devotedly to define those abs. The treadmill is her catwalk and it isn't just her denim that's ripped. Clothes are the vehicle she uses to draw attention to her body, which, great tits and glockenspiel-stomach notwithstanding, has all the allure of a piece of classical statuary.

CHECKLIST

LOCATION:

DATE:

DESCRIPTION:

OVERHEARD:

ACCESSORIES:

WANKER RATING

/ 10

ADDICTED TO Protein.

BRANDS Lululemon; New Balance; Calvin Klein Underwear; Sweaty Betty; Under Armour; Gymshark; 2XU; Goop; Nike; The North Face.

MANTRA/MOTTO Just do it.

WHAT NOT TO SAY TO THEM Aren't you out of proportion?

GODS Gisele Bündchen; The Rock; Tracy Anderson; J-Lo; Hugh Jackman.

ICONIC ITEM Leggings.

COLOURS Dark (they hide the sweat better).

TEXTILES Lycra.

ACCESSORIES Metal water bottle; incognito 'workout' cap; fluoro sneakers.

THE GYM BUNNY

Her hashtag is #eatcleantraindirty, and when she's not turning wholegrains into 'gains', her endorphin addiction makes them a click-bait gym bore. The style is relaxed and oversized. The only flesh you'll see is the ripple of abs under the crop top.

Incognito 'workout' cap

Smartphone, for taking endless selfies

Active hoodie

Crop top, exposing abs

Dark leggings

Colourful sneakers

MUST-HAVE ACCESSORY

'WORKOUT' CAP

THE NORTHERN INDEPENDENT

His day job may be selling EA7 tracksuits in Hull, but he still thinks he's the best thing to hit the street since the Wallabee. From his 9-to-5 behind-the-till to the football terraces then on to the pub, the Northern Independent is the archetypal Northern geezer who likes to think he's known for his 'threads'.

When he's flaunting his latest deliveries, it's all about authenticity, provenance and scarcity. He knows exactly what he likes, and everything is thoroughly considered: it's the subtle details that admit you to his club. An encyclopedic knowledge of authentic menswear classics, plus a studious approach to buying and evaluating brands, make the Northern Independent a connoisseur of timeless casual menswear. He'll suss you out by giving your outfit the once over – and he'll quickly establish whether you can join the club.

CHECKLIST

LOCATION:

DATE:

DESCRIPTION:

OVERHEARD:

ACCESSORIES:

WANKER RATING

/ 10

ADDICTED TO Being right.

BRANDS Fred Perry; Mephisto; Clarks Originals; Hikerdelic; Henri Lloyd; Kangol; Universal Works.

MANTRA/MOTTO Alright, our kid?

WHAT NOT TO SAY TO THEM Trouble at t'mill?

GODS Massimo Osti; The Gallagher Brothers; Tony Wilson; Peter Saville; The Smiths.

ICONIC ITEM The hooded windcheater.

COLOURS Burnt orange or French workwear blue.

TEXTILES Anything that's made in the UK.

ACCESSORIES Bucket hat; copy of the *NME* (R.I.P.); round John Lennon-type frames.

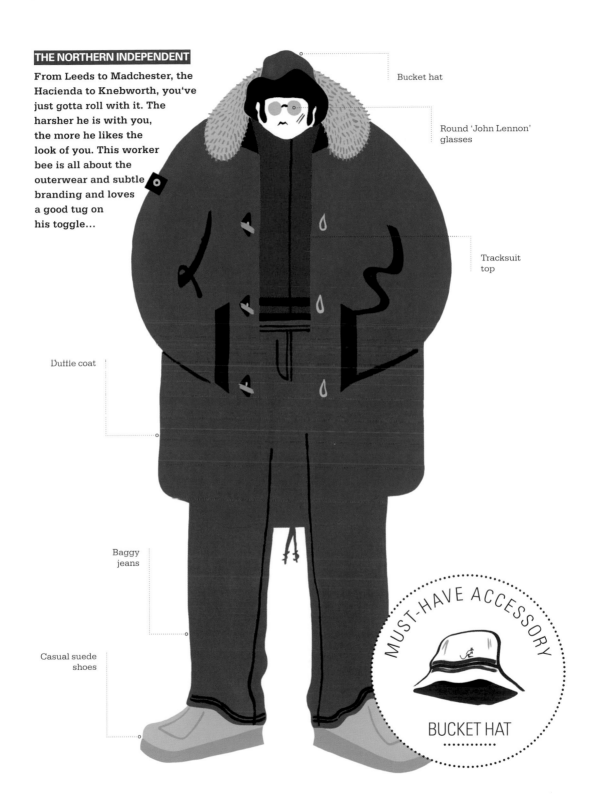

THE NORTHERN INDEPENDENT

From Leeds to Madchester, the Hacienda to Knebworth, you've just gotta roll with it. The harsher he is with you, the more he likes the look of you. This worker bee is all about the outerwear and subtle branding and loves a good tug on his toggle…

Bucket hat

Round 'John Lennon' glasses

Tracksuit top

Duffle coat

Baggy jeans

Casual suede shoes

MUST-HAVE ACCESSORY

BUCKET HAT

SPOT THE WANKER:
THE MAGPIE

More maven than raven, the Magpie is a cherry picker of beautiful pieces. From eBay to charity shops and from hand-me-downs to Bond Street, she's a real style kleptomaniac. Layers of chiffon, silk and tulle flutter and float around her like a tropical jellyfish in a typhoon. This is fashion as art, and the Magpie is a walking, talking masterpiece on a constant adventure involving colour, print and pattern.

She's the #FashionWankers' Bird of Paradise, a willowy doll in a post-boho whirlwind of influences drawn from her travels and experiences. Nothing matches and that's part of the point. Her wardrobe is mostly gifted – people queue up to dress the Magpie – and she thinks she's the style original. Don't mention that you last saw that dazzling dress on the sale rail at Anthropologie.

CHECKLIST

LOCATION:

....

DATE:

....

DESCRIPTION:

....

OVERHEARD:

....

ACCESSORIES:

....

WANKER RATING

/ 10

ADDICTED TO Vintage shops.

BRANDS Gucci; Marni; Dries Van Noten; Valentino; Liberty of London; Pucci; Simone Rocha.

MANTRA/MOTTO More is more.

WHAT NOT TO SAY TO THEM Does it come in black?

GODS Zandra Rhodes; Florence Welch; Iris Apfel; Lindsay Kemp; Oscar Wilde; Grayson Perry; Barbara Hulanicki.

ICONIC ITEM Her grandmother's fringed tablecloth, worn as a scarf.

COLOURS Baby pink, spring green, tangerine and turquoise. All at once.

TEXTILES Silk, chiffon and tulle.

ACCESSORIES Large sunglasses; printed Italian silk scarves; an exotic pet.

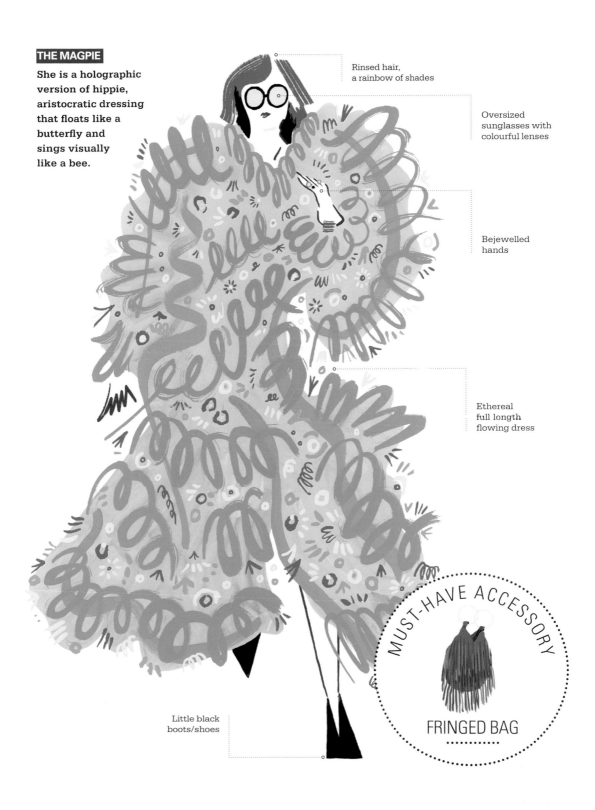

THE MAGPIE

She is a holographic version of hippie, aristocratic dressing that floats like a butterfly and sings visually like a bee.

Rinsed hair, a rainbow of shades

Oversized sunglasses with colourful lenses

Bejewelled hands

Ethereal full length flowing dress

Little black boots/shoes

MUST-HAVE ACCESSORY

FRINGED BAG

SPOT THE WANKER:
THE PARISIAN X-RAY

Rallying against the bourgeoisie as though it's 1968, this skinny wanker takes to the cobbled streets of Paris like the Beat Generation on a come-down. Starving himself on the babyfood diet, he has barely enough energy to smile, so he just drags on his Gauloises and sips his black coffee. Anything as long as it's black, in fact – the Parisian X-Ray is a string-bean vision. His chosen size is zero, and even then, the clothes, while skinny, aren't tight: the body has never seen exercise as muscles just get in the way.

This is timeless rock'n'roll style; silk scarves and wide hats. It just needs an acoustic guitar on a strategically slashed knee. A stylish ghost, these pale characters live life in monochrome and are dressed like party animals 24/7. Tu vois? *exhales smoke*.

CHECKLIST

LOCATION:
....

DATE:
....

DESCRIPTION:
....

OVERHEARD:
....

ACCESSORIES:
....

WANKER RATING

/ 10

ADDICTED TO Nicotine.

BRANDS Saint Laurent; Celine; The Kooples; Dior; Zadig & Voltaire.

MANTRA/MOTTO Live thin, die young.

WHAT NOT TO SAY TO THEM You need to eat more fruit.

GODS Hedi Slimane; Pete Doherty; Jack Kerouac; Stevie Nicks; Jane Birkin; Andy Warhol; Patti Smith; Robert Mapplethorpe.

ICONIC ITEM Black leather biker jacket.

COLOURS All the shades. So long as they're black.

TEXTILES Leather.

ACCESSORIES Wide-brimmed hat; silver necklaces, rings and bangles; skinny scarves with fringes.

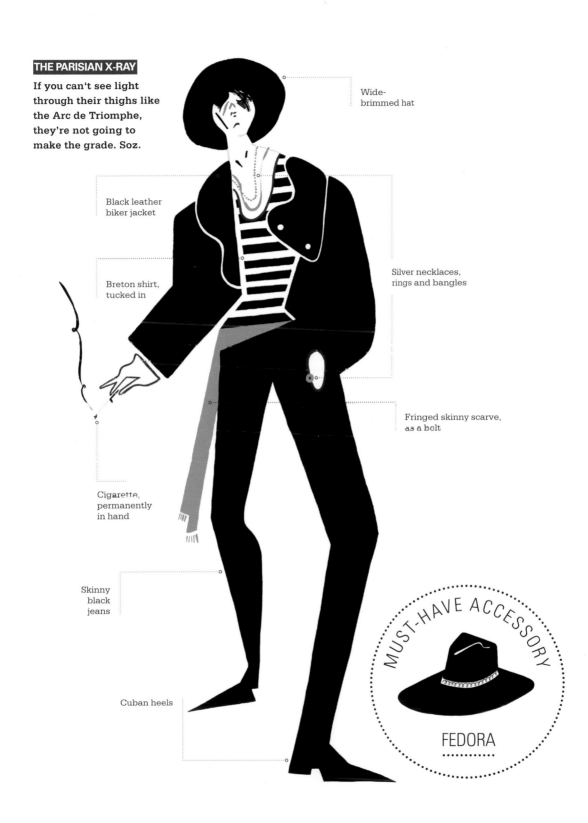

THE PARISIAN X-RAY

If you can't see light through their thighs like the Arc de Triomphe, they're not going to make the grade. Soz.

Wide-brimmed hat

Black leather biker jacket

Breton shirt, tucked in

Silver necklaces, rings and bangles

Fringed skinny scarve, as a belt

Cigarette, permanently in hand

Skinny black jeans

Cuban heels

MUST-HAVE ACCESSORY

FEDORA

SPOT THE WANKER:
THE METROPOLITAN ELITE

CHECKLIST

LOCATION:

DATE:

DESCRIPTION:

OVERHEARD:

ACCESSORIES:

WANKER RATING

/ 10

Only good vibes. The Metropolitan Elite, AKA the Woke Wanker, likes to buy organic and is flexi-vegan, depending on the restaurant. She's not quite so hung up on origin when she's WhatsApping her dealer at 2am.

Putting the mind into mindfulness, she's on a perpetual quest for a nirvana of wellness, although she was forced into a conscious uncoupling with hot yoga after finding out about its founder's indiscretions. Now, she alternates between cat or goat yoga, depending on the phases of the moon and the availability of the animals at the city farm.

She thinks it's important to share, but she never listens. Her spirit animal depends on her current documentary Netflix crush, and she's trying to acquire a taste for tap water after clocking the crashing carbon footprint of her favourite brand, Fiji. She's often seen reading the cartons in the health-food aisle, with furrowed brow.

ADDICTED TO Fermenting stuff.

BRANDS Folk; Goop; Raeburn; Everlane; People Tree; Stella McCartney; Finisterre; Ganni; Patagonia; Whole Foods.

MANTRA/MOTTO Stay woke.

WHAT NOT TO SAY TO THEM Can somebody explain 'white privilege'?

GODS Gwyneth Paltrow; Angelina Jolie; Nelson Mandela; Colin Kaepernick; Prince Harry.

ICONIC ITEM The fabric tote.

COLOURS The colours of the sunrise or sunset.

TEXTILES Organic bamboo.

ACCESSORIES Yoga mat; chakra spray; raffia bag, handwoven by artisans in Morocco.

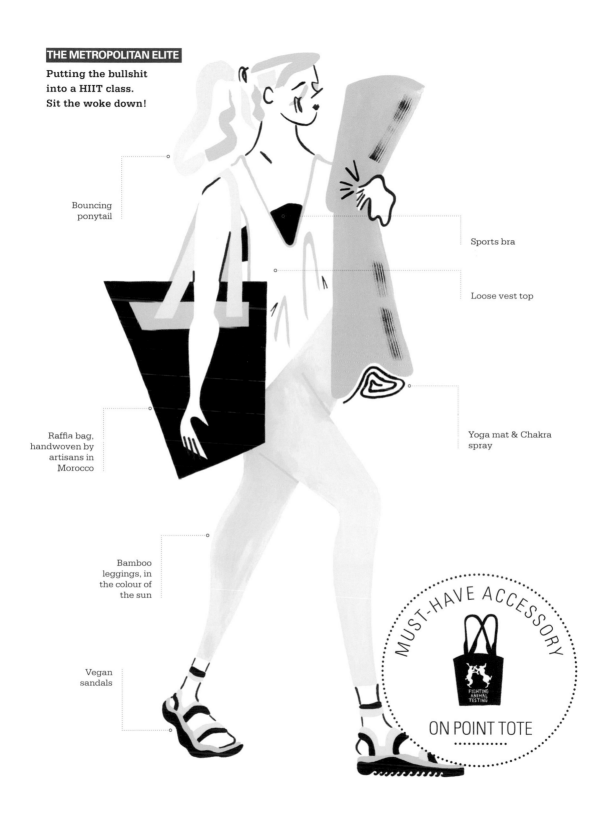

THE METROPOLITAN ELITE

**Putting the bullshit
into a HIIT class.
Sit the woke down!**

Bouncing
ponytail

Sports bra

Loose vest top

Raffia bag,
handwoven by
artisans in
Morocco

Yoga mat & Chakra
spray

Bamboo
leggings, in
the colour of
the sun

Vegan
sandals

MUST-HAVE ACCESSORY

FIGHTING
ANIMAL
TESTING

ON POINT TOTE

SPOT THE WANKER:
THE SNEAKER GEEK

With more drops than an ocean, the Sneaker Geek is a self-confessed sneakerhead, addicted to the latest footwear offerings from the hottest designers and sportswear companies. His inner hypebeast is the envy of his peer group – he's already wearing styles that everyone else has barely started to talk about and he gets maximum enjoyment from their envious stares as he bounces down the street.

He drives his own hype and is often intent on finding a mate to help bypass the queue for the latest drop or entering ballots for the chance to buy exclusives. He also heads out on unicorn hunts for dead stock. Elbow-deep in silica sachets, this collector is beyond precious about his sneakers. The fuglier the better. Box fresh for life.

CHECKLIST

LOCATION:

DATE:

DESCRIPTION:

OVERHEARD:

ACCESSORIES:

WANKER RATING

/ 10

ADDICTED TO New kicks.

BRANDS Jason Markk; Crep Protect; Supreme; BAPE; BBC; YMC; Nike; Adidas; Reebok; Puma.

MANTRA/MOTTO Don't crease 'em.

WHAT NOT TO SAY TO THEM Who's Michael Jordan?

GODS Raf Simons; Kanye West; Phil Knight; Bill Bowerman; Stan Smith.

HOLY GRAIL Nike MAG.

COLOURS Essex-smile white.

TEXTILES Italian leather.

ACCESSORIES Repel spray.

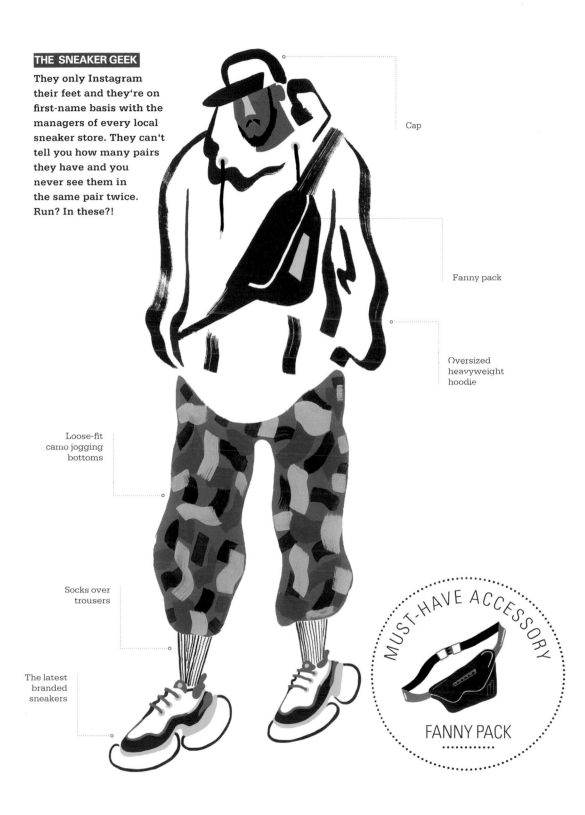

THE SNEAKER GEEK

They only Instagram their feet and they're on first-name basis with the managers of every local sneaker store. They can't tell you how many pairs they have and you never see them in the same pair twice. Run? In these?!

Cap

Fanny pack

Oversized heavyweight hoodie

Loose-fit camo jogging bottoms

Socks over trousers

The latest branded sneakers

MUST-HAVE ACCESSORY

FANNY PACK

THE DATED HIPSTER

What's going to happen when the beard turns grey, those tattoos fade and gin once again becomes a drink for grannies? Who knows, but the Dated Hipster doesn't care, because he isn't letting go of the full-beard-and-side-parting ensemble any time soon.

This beardy wanker is still busy drinking cloudy craft beer from chemistry beakers, eating burgers on Welsh slates and working in that Victorian-inspired barber shop like it's 2010.

The Dated Hipster puts the man into the manliest of stereotypes – according to him, he's been everything from fisherman to woodsman to game keep to cattle rancher and that's just on a trip to the local store. When not combing Brylcreem into their hair, they're trying to cook the perfect poached eggs and likes to support 'Independents' which all turn out to be owned by H&M.

CHECKLIST

LOCATION:

DATE:

DESCRIPTION:

OVERHEARD:

ACCESSORIES:

WANKER RATING

/ 10

ADDICTED TO Fresh vinyl and flat whites.

BRANDS Hiut Denim; All Saints; Urban Outfitters; Red Wing; Levi's; Vintage; Shinola; Arket; Woolrich.

MANTRA/MOTTO Is this certified organic?

WHAT NOT TO SAY TO THEM Tell me more about your tattoos.

GODS Joseph Gordon-Levitt; Shia LaBeouf; Michael Cera; Ricky Hall; Mischa Barton; Zooey Deschanel.

ICONIC ITEM Beard oil.

COLOURS Black and red checks (Buffalo).

TEXTILES Flannel.

ACCESSORIES Beard comb; sensible shoes; beanies; spectacles; braces/suspenders; pork pie hats.

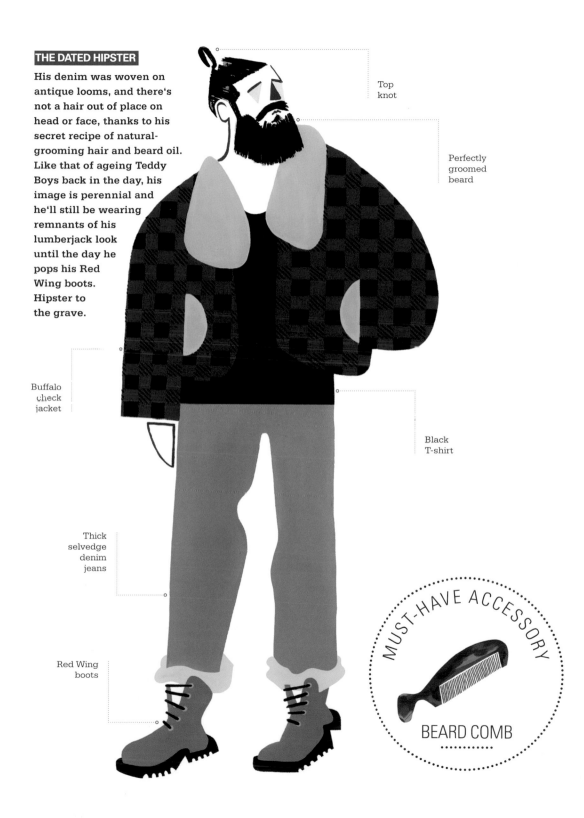

THE DATED HIPSTER

His denim was woven on antique looms, and there's not a hair out of place on head or face, thanks to his secret recipe of natural-grooming hair and beard oil. Like that of ageing Teddy Boys back in the day, his image is perennial and he'll still be wearing remnants of his lumberjack look until the day he pops his Red Wing boots. Hipster to the grave.

Top knot

Perfectly groomed beard

Buffalo check jacket

Black T-shirt

Thick selvedge denim jeans

Red Wing boots

MUST-HAVE ACCESSORY

BEARD COMB

SPOT THE WANKER:
THE SLOANE WANKER

Cast your mind back to Princess Diana as a shy nursery-school teacher and you'll catch a glimpse of the Sloane Wanker's natural predecessor. Forty years on, this horsey wanker has been happily stuck in her preppy rut since her godmother gave her the traditional silver spoon at her christening (at St Luke's & Christ Church, Chelsea, natch).

She disappeared to boarding school for her formative years, but now this forgotten about siren of polite society is ripe for a renaissance. Not since the 1990s has anything this exciting happened west of Park Lane; she's making the country look chic again. Marriage is the ultimate goal as it ever was – if a polo-playing prince or a stately-home-owning earl doesn't show up, then an investment banker will probably make the cut. It's OK to look posh again. Yah.

CHECKLIST

LOCATION:

DATE:

DESCRIPTION:

OVERHEARD:

ACCESSORIES:

WANKER RATING

/ 10

ADDICTED TO Horses and dogs.

BRANDS Unaccented Celine; Ralph Lauren; Barbour; John Lewis; Temperley; Jack Wills; Hermès; Russell & Bromley.

MANTRA/MOTTO There were three of us in this marriage. *looks up*

WHAT NOT TO SAY TO THEM What's the difference between a public and a private School?

GODS Lady Diana Spencer; Princess Anne; Kate Middleton; Alexa Chung.

ICONIC ITEM Pussy-bow blouse.

COLOURS Coffee and cream.

TEXTILES Harris Tweed.

ACCESSORIES Cross-body bag; riding boots; pearl necklace; vintage Hermès scarves.

THE SLOANE WANKER

More Colefax & Fowler than Dolce & Gabbana, if you can't shoot it, wear it or eat it, then she's simply not interested. Rah!

'Natural'-looking hairstyle

Pussy-bow blouse

Barbour coat

Harris tweed trousers

Hunter wellies

MUST-HAVE ACCESSORY

PEARL NECKLACE

SPOT THE WANKER:
THE ALOOF EDITOR

Worked at *Vogue*, but had a bigger relationship with DHL than YSL, not that anybody's EVER to know that... The Aloof Editor lives and dies on the choices they make, even if nobody reads their soon-to-be defunct biannual magazine. Their whole life is an edit of the fashion world, overthinking their look and knowing fashion's VVIPs.

Air-kissing arses to get the plummiest jobs, the Aloof Editor has an encyclopedic knowledge of fashion history and *Sex & The City* and knows each and every fashion brand's Creative Director, the more obscure the better.

Judge and be judged, she plonks herself down in the frow at fashion weeks, never makes eye contact and wears the latest 'gifted' designer bag high and across the body. She won't commit to talking to you until she's exhausted all other options and decided you're the best of a bad bunch.

CHECKLIST

LOCATION:

DATE:

DESCRIPTION:

OVERHEARD:

ACCESSORIES:

WANKER RATING

/ 10

ADDICTED TO Free stuff.

BRANDS Simone Rocha; Christopher Kane; Erdem; Old Céline; Jacquemus; Marine Serre.

MANTRA/MOTTO Nothing tastes as good as skinny feels.

WHAT NOT TO SAY TO THEM You've got a standing ticket.

GODS Diana Vreeland; Anna Wintour; Grace Coddington; Carmel Snow; Truman Capote; Condé Montrose Nast; Kate Moss.

ICONIC ITEM Dark oversized sunglasses.

COLOURS Ask to Pantone, I haven't got time for this...

TEXTILES Fun fur.

ACCESSORIES Designer samples or anything 'gifted by the designer'.

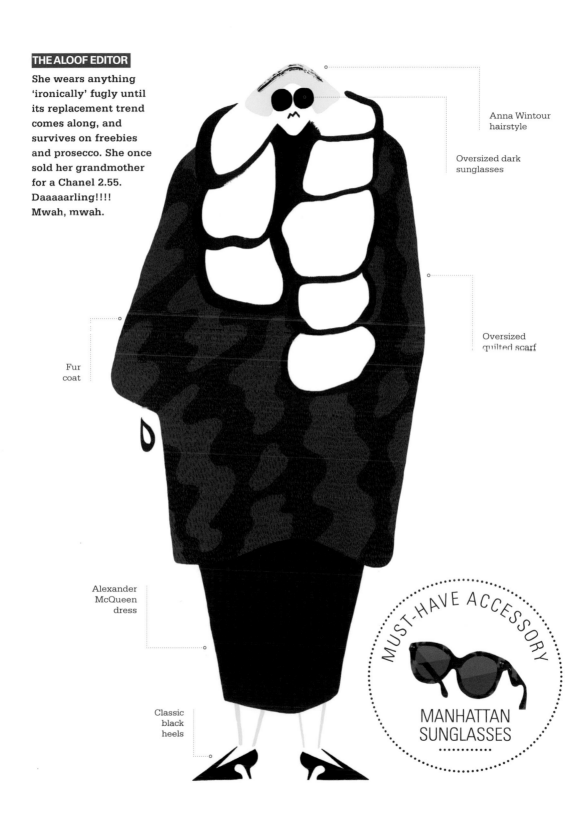

THE ALOOF EDITOR

She wears anything
'ironically' fugly until
its replacement trend
comes along, and
survives on freebies
and prosecco. She once
sold her grandmother
for a Chanel 2.55.
Daaaaarling!!!!
Mwah, mwah.

Anna Wintour
hairstyle

Oversized dark
sunglasses

Oversized
quilted scarf

Fur
coat

Alexander
McQueen
dress

Classic
black
heels

MUST-HAVE ACCESSORY

MANHATTAN
SUNGLASSES

THE GLOBAL TRAVELLER

This rolling stone gathers no moss, touching down in more countries than Zara. She's 'dropped out' of mainstream fashion by pretending she doesn't really care what she looks like while at the same time flashing her washboard stomach and 'naturally' highlighted hair all over social media.

Life is one long gap year and there are suspicions of Trustafarian status. Her VW camper makes a Maybach look economical, and for all its Scooby Doo realness she's not exactly roughing it on those trips to Cornwall or Ibiza or Kerala or Bali…(you get the idea).

Mentally, she keeps her environmental footprint light, while racking up thousands of miles on budget airlines. The only sport she does is plogging – picking up trash while jogging – down on yet another white sandy beach.

Her new 'thang' is tap water, and all her accessories are souvenirs handmade by local 'artisans' while surreptitiously peeling off the 'Made In China' stickers.

CHECKLIST

LOCATION:

DATE:

DESCRIPTION:

OVERHEARD:

ACCESSORIES:

WANKER RATING

/ 10

ADDICTED TO 'Experiences'.

BRANDS Keen; Teva; Malibu Sandals; S'well; Hydro Flask; Arc'teryx; Patagonia; Columbia; People Tree; Eastpak; Thule; Toms.

MANTRA/MOTTO Here we go again…

WHAT NOT TO SAY TO THEM Turn right.

GODS David Attenborough; Anita Roddick; Jack Dorsey; Kate Hudson.

ICONIC ITEM The bashed-up rucksack with yoga/sleeping mat.

COLOURS Rainbow of colours bleeding into each other.

TEXTILES Kente; Batik; Ikat.

ACCESSORIES Ankle bracelet; large straw hat; Teva sandals.

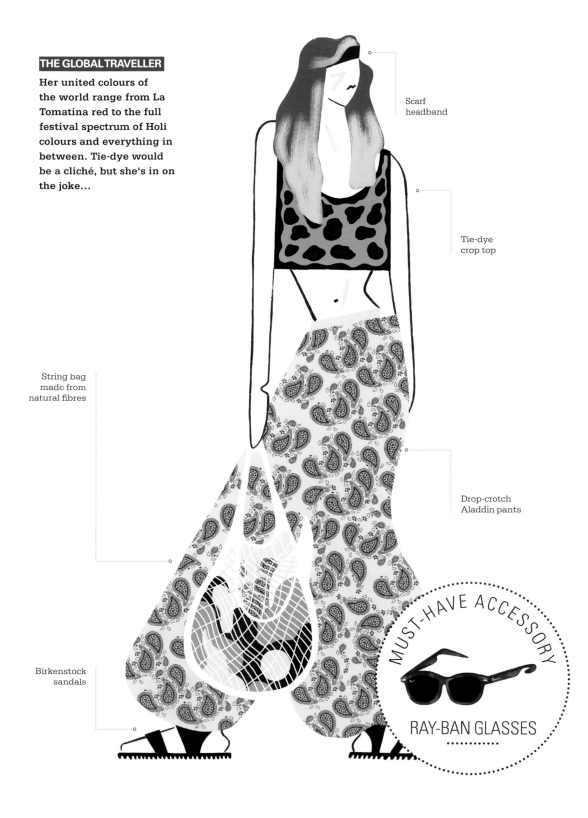

THE GLOBAL TRAVELLER

Her united colours of the world range from La Tomatina red to the full festival spectrum of Holi colours and everything in between. Tie-dye would be a cliché, but she's in on the joke…

Scarf headband

Tie-dye crop top

String bag made from natural fibres

Drop-crotch Aladdin pants

Birkenstock sandals

MUST-HAVE ACCESSORY

RAY-BAN GLASSES

WHICH WANKER
R U?

Are you on Instagram?

YES → Are you already over this?

YES → You're a KNOW-IT-ALL

NO → Have your clothes still got the labels on?

NO → Is Hedi Slimane king?

YES → You're an PARISIAN X-RAY

NO

DO YOU SMILE?

NO

YES → Was there life before social media?

YES → Are your clothes older than you?

YES → Do you live or want to live in West London?

YES

NO

NO → You're a DATED HIPSTER

NO → Is fashion your life?

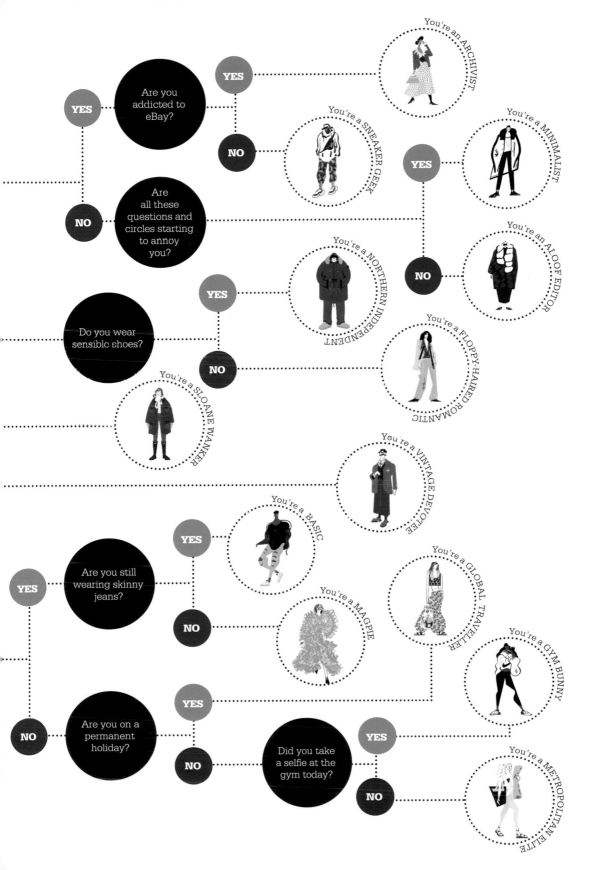

YES — Are you addicted to eBay?

YES — You're an ARCHIVIST

NO — You're a SNEAKER GEEK

NO — Are all these questions and circles starting to annoy you?

YES — You're a MINIMALIST

NO — You're an ALOOF EDITOR

Do you wear sensible shoes?

YES — You're a NORTHERN INDEPENDENT

NO — You're a FLOPPY-HAIRED ROMANTIC

You're a SLOANE WANKER

You're a VINTAGE DEVOTEE

Are you still wearing skinny jeans?

YES — You're a BASIC

NO — You're a MAGPIE

You're a GLOBAL TRAVELLER

You're a GYM BUNNY

YES — **NO** — Are you on a permanent holiday?

YES — Did you take a selfie at the gym today?

YES — You're a METROPOLITAN ELITE

NO —

ULTIMATE FASHION WANKER
QUOTES

Fashion history is peppered with the fabulous trying to define what fashion and style means to them. Take note of these soundbites from these icons of style. #FashionWankers wise words indeed. Now, what would you say?

"THE JOY OF DRESSING IS AN ART."
—John Galliano

"IN ORDER TO BE IRREPLACEABLE ONE MUST ALWAYS BE DIFFERENT." —Coco Chanel

"TO ACHIEVE THE NONCHALANCE WHICH IS ABSOLUTELY NECESSARY FOR A MAN, ONE ARTICLE AT LEAST MUST NOT MATCH."
—Hardy Amies

"I CAN'T CONCENTRATE IN FLATS."
—Victoria Beckham

"WE'RE ALL BORN NAKED AND THE REST IS DRAG." —RuPaul

"THE BEST THINGS IN LIFE ARE FREE. THE SECOND BEST ARE VERY EXPENSIVE."
—Coco Chanel

"FASHIONS FADE, STYLE IS ETERNAL."
—Yves Saint Laurent

"IF PEOPLE TURN TO LOOK AT YOU ON THE STREET, YOU ARE NOT WELL DRESSED, BUT EITHER TOO STIFF, TOO TIGHT, OR TOO FASHIONABLE." —Beau Brummell

"IF YOU CAN'T BE BETTER THAN YOUR COMPETITION, JUST DRESS BETTER."
—Anna Wintour

"I'LL STOP WEARING BLACK WHEN THEY MAKE A DARKER COLOUR." Wednesday Addams

"FASHION IS LIKE EATING, YOU SHOULDN'T STICK TO THE SAME MENU." —Kenzo Takada

"YOU CAN NEVER BE OVERDRESSED OR OVEREDUCATED." —Oscar Wilde

"FASHION SHOULD BE A FORM OF ESCAPISM, AND NOT A FORM OF IMPRISONMENT." —Alexander McQueen

"I'M JUST TRYING TO CHANGE THE WORLD, ONE SEQUIN AT A TIME." —Lady Gaga

"FASHION WASN'T WHAT YOU WORE SOMEPLACE ANYMORE; IT WAS THE WHOLE REASON FOR GOING." —Andy Warhol

"I LOATHE NARCISSISM, BUT I APPROVE OF VANITY." —Diana Vreeland

121

FASHION WANKER
WORKBOOK

Fashion Wankers never stick within the lines, well, that's me being metaphorical, but when colouring in, it's best to try. Find your inner fashion designer and let the stresses of being so fabulous run out through your fingers. Here are some pages for you to design your own Fashion Wankers. When you've finished, upload to your social media platform of choice with the hashtag #FashionWankers. So, pick up those pens and pencils, flex those designer muscles and get involved.

DON'T COLOUR ME BAD; COLOUR ME GOOD

SPOT THE FASHION WANKER

INDEX

127

First published 2019 by
Ammonite Press
an imprint of Guild of Master Craftsman Publications Ltd
Castle Place, 166 High Street, Lewes, East Sussex
BN7 1XU, United Kingdom
www.ammonitepress.com

Publisher: Jason Hook
Design Manager: Robin Shields
Designer: Wayne Blades
Editor: Jamie Pumfrey
Illustrator: Oscar Mitchell

Colour reproduction by GMC Reprographics
Printed and bound in China

ACKNOWLEDGMENTS

Lezza-Ann for always encouraging me &
The Fashion Boys' WhatsApp Mafia.

PICTURE CREDITS

Shutterstock/Sashkovna: 4, 10, 32, 78, 82;
Berry2046: 6, 8; Rawpixel.com: 14t; Dmitry
Kalinovsky:16; FashionStock.com: 23r, 25cl,
50; Dean Drobot: 25l; zhangjin_net: 25cr;
Leavector: 27; Luchino: 35tl, 35tcr, 35tr, 35cr,
35bl, 35bcl, 35bcr; Mauro Del Signore: 35tcl,
35c; Huang Zheng: 35tc; Creative Lab: 35cl,
35ccl; Ferruccio Dall'Aglio: 35ccr; DKSStyle:
35br; RaDoll: 37; Nito: 39; PicoStudio: 43;
CatwalkPhotos: 45; Wavebreakmedia: 47;
Koyash07: 49; Jan Zahradka: 53; Kzww: 54;
Andrea Raffin: 56; Helen89: 60; Shelly Still
Photo: 62; Andersphoto: 65l, 65cl, 65r; Tinxi:
65cr; Balta Mihaita Sorin: 68r; Guteksk7: 69;
Color Symphony: 70; Oligo22: 72; Brilliantist
Studio: 76; Anastasia Lembrik: 84; Jiri
Vaclavek: 123. **Base London and The
Chic Geek**: 2, 12, 14l, 24, 29, 30l, 41, 42, 44,
55, 58, 63, 66, 68l, 71t, 84. **Oscar Mitchell**:
cover, 2, 14, 26, 30r, 34, 46, gatefold, 85, 87,
89, 91, 93, 95, 97, 99, 101, 103, 105, 107,
109, 111, 113, 115, 117, 118, 119. **Jeff
Sheldon**: 15l. **Lauren Richmond**: 15c.
**Library of Congress Prints and
Photographs Division Washington,
D.C.**: 19r. **Leslie Greaves**: 20l. **Alamy
Stock Photo**/Granger Historical Picture
Archive: 20r; Colaimages: 21l; Everett
Collection Inc: 22r; MediaPunch Inc:
23l; Pictorial Press Ltd: 57tl; Moviestore
Collection Ltd: 57tr; PictureLux/The
Hollywood Archive: 57ct; AF Archive:
57r, 57cb, 75; Allstar Picture Library: 57l;
Keystone Press: 57bl; Tanja-vashchuk: 57br;
World History Archive: 71b. **Nationaal
Archief**/Spaarnestad Photo: 21r.
Riksarkivet (National Archives of Norway):
22l. **Dom Hill**: 25r. **Noah Buscher**: 31.

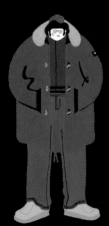

How was the book?
Please post your
feedback and photos:
#fashionwankers

AMMONITE
PRESS

www.ammonitepress.com